The Quotable Calvin Coolidge

Sensible Words for a New Century

President Calvin Coolidge, October 22, 1924

THE QUOTABLE CALVIN COOLIDGE

Sensible Words for a New Century

Compiled and Edited by Peter Hannaford

Images from the Past
Bennington, Vermont

1 2 3 4 5 6 7 8 9 10 XXX 08 07 06 05 04 03 02 01

Library of Congress Cataloging-in-Publication Data

Coolidge, Calvin, 1872-1933
    The Quotable Calvin Coolidge: sensible words for a new
century/compiled and edited by Peter Hannaford.

                    p. cm.

    Includes bibliographical references.

    ISBN 1-884592-33-3

    1. Coolidge, Calvin, 1872-1933—Quotations.
    2. United States—Politics and government—1923-1929
    —Quotations, maxims, etc. 3. United States—Politics
    and government—Quotations, maxims, etc. I. Hannaford,
    Peter. II. Title.

    E742.5.C76 2001.
    973.91'5'092—dc21

                        00—011423

Copyright© 2001 Peter Hannaford
Published by Images from the Past, Inc.
P.O. Box 137, Bennington, VT 05201
Tordis Ilg Isselhardt, Publisher
www.ImagesfromthePast.com
Printed in the United States of America
Project Editor: Stuart Murray
Design and Production:
        Ron Toelke Associates, Chatham, NY
Printer: Thomson-Shore, Inc., Dexter, MI

Dedicated to
the memory of
Calvin Coolidge

Thirtieth President of the
United States of America

"a good and a kindly man"

Acknowledgments

My thanks go to Cynthia Bittinger, executive director of the Calvin Coolidge Memorial Foundation, and her staff for their prompt and cheerful response to my requests for verification of many quotations and for their encouragement and support.

I am grateful, also, for the help of Jim Cooke, enactor of a highly regarded one-man show about Calvin Coolidge.

Staff members of the Library of Congress were helpful on many occasions, responding to my inquiries about source materials.

Tordis Ilg Isselhardt, president of Images from the Past, my publisher, provided encouragement, enthusiasm, and fascinating insights into the Vermont of the Thirtieth President.

My wife, Irene, as with my other books, carefully read the manuscript to make necessary corrections. Beyond that, she was, as always, an inspiration.

Table of Contents

Preface

Shortly after he took office as the Fortieth President of the United States, Ronald Reagan hung Calvin Coolidge's picture in the Cabinet Room of the White House. This did not surprise me. Having been closely associated with Reagan for a number of years, I knew that Coolidge, the Thirtieth President, was a favorite of his.

In several ways they were alike. Both believed in the value of work and self-reliance. Both believed that government intervention reduced individual freedom. Both believed that high tax rates inhibited economic growth. For national defense, both believed in what Reagan came to call "peace through strength." Both believed in the importance of language to communicate ideas effectively and to provide leadership. And, both had a deep faith in God.

When, in August 1981, the air traffic controllers' union announced it would call an illegal strike, President Reagan declared that if the controllers were not back on the job within forty-eight hours, they would forfeit their jobs. Most stayed out and were terminated. Many times in his public life, Reagan had stated that government employees could not strike against public safety. His inspiration for this was Coolidge's handling of the Boston police strike of 1919, during which— as Massachusetts governor—he sent a telegram to labor leader Samuel Gompers, saying, "There is no right to strike against the public safety by anybody, anywhere, at any time."

After four books on President Reagan, I wrote about another of his favorite predecessors, George Washington. Upon completing that book, I turned to President Coolidge, who has only recently begun to get the reappraisal he deserves.

There are some strong parallels between Coolidge's era and ours: great prosperity, general peace in the world, inventiveness, and scientific advances. As I began to review his written and spoken words, I found most of them strikingly applicable to today. His statements about radio and then-fledgling television—with appropriate word changes—would do for our era of VCRs, satellites, and broadband communications. We consider the effects of large political campaign contributions and of globalization to be current issues, but Coolidge was there first, as his quotations on these subjects show. Coolidge believed in—and practiced—lean, direct, clear prose. It is unadorned, thus giving it power. Unlike the poll-driven banalities and hyperbole practiced by many latter-day politicians, Coolidge gives it to us straight.

That was how he lived his life, as witnessed by a remark made soon after he died in 1933, by Miss Aurora Pierce, long-time housekeeper in the family homestead at Plymouth Notch. Calvin Coolidge had displayed the very finest qualities of state and national leadership, yet Miss Pierce described him simply and appropriately as "a good and kindly man."

Peter Hannaford
Washington, D.C.
July 2000

Introduction

On January 6, 1933, the day after Calvin Coolidge
died, humorist Will Rogers wrote this in his newspaper column:

> Mr. Coolidge you didn't have to die
> for me to throw flowers on your grave.
> I have told a million jokes about you,
> but every one was based on some of your
> splendid qualities. You had a hold on the
> American people regardless of politics.
> They knew you were honest, economical
> and had a native common sense.
> History generally records a place for
> a man who is ahead of his time. But, we
> that lived with you remember you
> because you was WITH your times.
> By golly, you little red-headed New
> Englander, I liked you. You put horse
> sense into statesmanship.

"Common sense," "horse sense"—these were
the distillations of Coolidge's New England
Yankee ancestry and upbringing. In 1781, his

great-great-grandfather, John Coolidge, had cleared land in the beautiful, small valley that is Plymouth Notch, Vermont. A captain in the Revolutionary War, John Coolidge had come from Massachusetts.

It was there in Plymouth Notch that John Calvin Coolidge was born on the Fourth of July, 1872 (he later dropped his first name). His boyhood centered on the family farm on that thin soil of Vermont, with its sharp winters. His world was that of the farm, the village church, the one-room school, and the village store, of which his father, also John Coolidge, was proprietor.

With loving parents and many relatives nearby, young Calvin had every reason to be a happy boy; his mother died, however, when he was twelve, and his sister died at age fifteen. His father remarried, and Calvin grew close to his stepmother. From his early experiences, a shyness grew in him which never left him.

Coolidge learned the Yankee virtues of self-reliance, thrift, and modesty. It was said that he had an almost sacramental view of the democracy of the town meeting. He learned to live with the changing rhythms of nature and, for the rest of his life, thought of Plymouth Notch as "home."

For his high school years, Calvin Coolidge attended Black River Academy in Ludlow,

Vermont, where he boarded. There, he gave the first speech of his life, on the historical importance of oratory. Graduating in May 1890, he went that fall to Amherst, Massachusetts, to take the Amherst College entrance examination. On the way he had caught a cold which interfered with his examination plans. He returned home to recover. In the late winter of 1890-91 he returned briefly to Black River Academy, but was encouraged by the school to go to St. Johnsbury Academy, Vermont's leading preparatory school, for review courses. In the spring of 1891 he earned a certificate from St. Johnsbury, which made him eligible to enter the freshman class at Amherst that fall.

At that liberal arts college he took Greek, Latin, mathematics, and rhetoric. He was most deeply influenced by his professor of philosophy, Charles E. Garman, who was legendary at Amherst. Garman used no textbooks, but taught from pamphlets he printed himself. He taught his students that ethical behavior and religious faith lay at the heart of a successful life. His idealism, intellectual curiosity, and sense of fairness captivated the young Coolidge.

Coolidge was not athletic, concentrating instead on his studies. In his junior year he shared with another student the J. Wesley Ladd prize for public speaking. As a senior, he co-founded the Amherst chapter of Phi Gamma Delta fraternity.

At graduation time, he was selected to give the "Grove Speech," a satire on college life. Thus, his wry wit came fully into play. Among his classmates were Dwight Morrow, who had a brilliant career on Wall Street and later became ambassador to Mexico, and Harlan Stone, who became chief justice of the United States Supreme Court. Throughout his life, Coolidge maintained ties with college classmates and attended many alumni gatherings.

By his senior year, young Coolidge had decided that the law was the profession he wished to pursue. Rather than apply to a law school, he decided to "read law" at a law firm. In due course, his contacts led him to the firm of Hammond and Field in the nearby county seat of Northampton, Massachusetts. He was invited to become a clerk there and did so in September 1895. Two and a half years later, he opened his own law office.

In October 1904, Coolidge married Grace Goodhue of Burlington, Vermont, a woman of poise, charm, and good humor. A recent graduate of the University of Vermont, she had come to Northampton to take a training course to teach the deaf.

Beginning with his appointment to the Northampton Republican city committee in 1897, Coolidge began a long, patient climb up the political ladder. Effusive glad-handing was alien to him. His succinct way of saying things, and his demonstrations of "common sense" were what impressed people. His almost mystical belief in the value of public service grew as his political career advanced. His combination of cautiousness and modesty made it necessary for him to feel he had to be fully prepared for the next step before taking it. Studying the political rise of Calvin Coolidge, one could also conclude that he was shrewd.

In succession, Coolidge was elected to the city council, named city solicitor, appointed county clerk of the courts, chaired the Republican city committee, was elected to the state House of Representatives, elected mayor of Northampton, elected to the state senate, elected president of the senate, elected lieutenant governor and then governor of Massachusetts, then vice president of the United States. Between 1898 and 1924, he faced the voters twenty times and won nineteen contests (losing only a race for the Northampton school committee in 1905).

When President Warren Harding died in August 1923, it was as if Calvin Coolidge had been made for the times over which he was to preside. Untainted by the scandals that emanated from the Harding Administration (Harding himself was not involved in them), Coolidge methodically created an administration that was intended to fuel economic growth. Unparalleled prosperity followed.

Yet, Coolidge was so "with" his own time—a time suddenly supplanted by a worldwide Depression—that he was not long in his grave before tribunes of the New Deal and historians sympathetic to it had relegated his memory to a pigeonhole labeled "failure."

It is as true in politics as in war that the victors get to write the history. Franklin D. Roosevelt and his New Deal supporters had a political interest in consigning what they called the "Harding-Coolidge-Hoover Era" to political purgatory. They naturally wanted to keep their hold on political power, so they lumped FDR's three predecessors together and discredited them all for the ills of the Depression in order to achieve that aim.

As a result, there soon developed a Calvin Coolidge stereotype. Among the characterizations were these: he was cold, disliked people, worshiped wealth, was unconcerned about ordinary people, was obsessively materialistic, was listless, unimaginative, inactive, crabbed and narrow in outlook, lacked intellectual curiosity, knew little about history, and had no sense of humor.

In a trenchant paper delivered at a 1998 Coolidge conference at the John F. Kennedy Library in Cambridge, Massachusetts, the library's historian, Sheldon M. Stern, Ph.D, said,

"The conventional wisdom on the Thirtieth President is anchored in two books," biographies of Coolidge by William Allen White.

White was a journalist, editor of the Emporia, Kansas, *Gazette* (he liked the sobriquet "The Sage of Emporia"), and was widely published in national magazines. He was also an active Republican, attending several conventions as a delegate. He first came to national attention with an anti-Populist tract which boosted the McKinley campaign over William Jennings Bryan.

Not long after Theodore Roosevelt occupied the White House, White became a Progressive, favoring government intervention to cure various social ills. By 1912, when Roosevelt bolted the Republican party and ran as a Bull Moose (resulting in President Taft's loss to Woodrow Wilson), White stood with him. White later returned to the Republican party and supported Harding, Coolidge, and Hoover.

Nevertheless, by 1938, when White wrote his second biography of Coolidge, *A Puritan in Babylon,* he had decidedly mixed views about the Thirtieth President. He liked Coolidge personally, but he saw him as a throwback to an earlier time in the nation's history, ill-suited to changing modern times, and blind to the possibility that prosperity could not last.

Coolidge critics for years jeered at the quotation "The business of America is business." Here was proof to them that Coolidge worshiped Mammon and commerce over all else and was materialistic. Unfortunately for them, for later generations, and for the truth, this is a misquote by White. Coolidge actually said, in a 1925 speech to the American Society of Newspaper Editors, "After all, the chief business of the American people is business." This was in a context in which he discussed both the news and business aspects of newspapers and how they related to the people. He had stated accurately that most people were chiefly concerned with the daily business of their lives.

In the same speech, Coolidge made it clear— as he had done many times before—that material wealth is only a means to an end, such as for "the multiplication of schools, the increase of knowledge, the dissemination of intelligence, the encouragement of science, the broadening of outlook, the expansion of liberties, the widening of culture."

In his books and in several articles, White misquoted Coolidge time and again, whether inadvertently or not. The misquote became embedded in the Coolidge stereotype. Along with criticism of Coolidge, however, White did not stint in praise of his subject. White praised him for his honesty, frugality, cautious and deliberate approach to problems, for his idealism and his commitment to service. He understood Coolidge's shyness and its sources (the simple, austere Vermont farm life, the early death of his mother and sister) and describes him as "an affectionate and aspiring man terribly repressed."

White understood that Coolidge sought to overcome his shyness through his "belief in the sacramental character of public service."

For years, Roosevelt biographers and New Deal historians cherry-picked White's criticisms of Coolidge, using the negatives and ignoring his sympathetic and positive comments. And for years, Coolidge's name could not be mentioned in a speech by a Republican politician—so thoroughly had he been stereotyped as a failed president, and a slightly comic figure ("Silent Cal") at that.

One of the first signs of change was when Marvin Stone, editor-in-chief of *U.S. News & World Report,* devoted his July 4, 1980, editorial to Coolidge, in effect calling for a reappraisal of the Thirtieth President, whom he described as "much maligned." Stone's next five Independence Day editorials were devoted to this task. Meanwhile, in early 1981, newly inaugurated President Ronald Reagan hung a Coolidge portrait in the Cabinet Room of the White House. This made news. Then, in August that year,

Reagan's swift and decisive handling of the air traffic controllers' strike brought comparisons with Coolidge's handling of the Boston police strike of 1919.

In 1982, Thomas B. Silver's book, *Coolidge and the Historians*, dissected the by-then conventional wisdom of major historians such as Henry Steele Commager, Allan Nevins, and especially Arthur Schlesinger, Jr., who had taken White's negative comments at face value and ignored the positive ones. Silver concluded: "In the hands of a historian like Arthur Schlesinger, Jr., history becomes a weapon. It is wielded in the fight to advance a political cause." In this case, the cause was active government intervention to solve virtually all problems—or "statism," as critics label it.

Then, in July 1998, the Kennedy Library invited nineteen historians, commentators, and students of the Coolidge era to deliver papers to a conference entitled "Calvin Coolidge: Examining the Evidence." The conference attracted considerable—and serious—media attention. The reconsideration of Coolidge was thus fully under way.

Coolidge was not without his faults, but the stereotypical criticisms of him said more about the ideological bent of his New Deal–era historian critics than they did about him. His record as a legislator and as lieutenant governor and governor in Massachusetts is that of a man who favored fiscal prudence and self-reliance for most people, but help for those who needed it. He was considered a "progressive" on a number of issues. He supported legislation to stop price-fixing. He was for women's suffrage and the direct election of U.S. senators. He favored adequate funding for welfare and for the state's hospitals for the mentally ill. He supported measures to improve workplace safety, to increase the number of playgrounds for children, and to provide special, low railway fares for workers and their children.

Throughout his public life in Massachusetts, Coolidge gained a good deal of support from laboring men and women. He believed ardently in the dignity and value of labor. He came by this belief naturally, from his childhood on the farm, where he learned to give up his seat in the family wagon whenever the hard-working farm hand was to go on the journey. As Massachusetts governor, he enacted a bill to reduce the work week to forty-eight hours for women and children. He also enacted bills to increase all workers' compensation payments and to include compensation for those with partial disabilities. He was instrumental in passing laws that restricted the size of rent increases, and he appointed a commission to investigate and report its recommendations on maternity leave.

All these were considered "progressive" measures at the time.

Radical movements swept Europe in the wake of World War I. Governor Coolidge was worried by the increasing clamor for radicalism in the United States. Much of his rhetoric and many of his actions as governor were intended to implement reforms in order to lessen the appeal of radical proposals, for he was a believer in improving the institutions of society rather than destroying them.

His handling of the Boston police strike of September 1919 thrust him into the national consciousness. Involved were his long experience of carefully analyzing a situation before acting, coupled with his respect for law, order, and the institutions of society.

Coolidge was sympathetic with the plight of the police, who worked eighty to ninety hours a week, and had poor working conditions and poor pay. In his 1929 autobiography, he wrote, "I do not approve of any strike. But can you blame the police for feeling as they do when they get less than a street car conductor?"

Early in 1919, Governor Coolidge had quietly sent an emissary to the American Woolen Company in Lawrence, Massachusetts, to monitor a strike. The governor was being pressured to send in the State Guard to break the strike. His emissary recommended against it. Coolidge privately urged the management of the textile company to settle the strike at the bargaining table. They finally did, and the strike ended peacefully on May 20th.

In 1919, Boston's police commissioner was Edwin U. Curtis, a former mayor. Curtis, who was considered to be a man of integrity, but stubborn, had been appointed in December 1918 by Coolidge's predecessor. While, under Massachusetts law, the governor appointed Boston's police commissioner, the commissioner could change neither the size of the police force nor its pay scale without the mayor's approval.

When a group of police officers formed a "club" within the force to obtain a union charter from the American Federation of Labor, Curtis issued an order forbidding any member of the force from joining a union. The order was ignored. Curtis charged the eight leaders of the new police union with insubordination. The union warned him that if its leaders were disciplined, they would go on strike. Curtis proceeded to prosecute the eight leaders, and then eleven more. They were found guilty, but he postponed their sentencing for ten days, to give them time to recant. Boston's mayor, Andrew J. Peters, a Democrat, took Curtis's side in the matter, but was more inclined to compromise.

Governor Coolidge took the position that, in

this case, the rules could not be arbitrated. Police were public-safety officers and, in the interest of maintaining civil order, strikes by police could not be permitted. He took a strictly legal approach to the separation of powers, believing that he must not interfere in the commissioner's work.

Commissioner Curtis postponed sentencing until Monday, September 8th. Meanwhile, over the weekend, a "blue-ribbon" citizens' committee reported its recommendation that the nineteen officers not be disciplined, that no strike be called, and that an arbitration board be created to deal with grievances. Mayor Peters supported the report. Nevertheless, on Monday morning, Curtis suspended the nineteen policemen. The mayor and the chairman of the citizens' group asked Coolidge to mobilize state troops in the event of the strike. Characteristic of him, Coolidge declined on the ground that Commissioner Curtis had assured him he could and would handle the situation.

The Boston police force voted to strike at the end of the next day, Tuesday, September 9th. Coolidge offered Curtis the State Guard, but the police commissioner declined the offer. Curtis assured the governor the situation was under control. But by a little after 5 p.m., a substantial number of police officers had walked off the job.

Two troops of the State Guard had their regularly scheduled drill that evening, but they were dismissed when it appeared all was quiet. By late evening, however, vandals and looters were breaking into stores, and rioting ensued. Curtis had been too trusting of advice from his staff.

Coolidge later wrote, "I have always felt that I should have called out the State Guard as soon as the police left their posts. The Commissioner did not feel that this was necessary."

On Wednesday, Mayor Peters called out Boston's State Guard unit and asked Coolidge to call out three more regiments from elsewhere in the state. Police officers who had not gone on strike were joined by citizen volunteers to create an ad hoc police force. (Media and public opinion were strongly opposed to the strikers.) Order was restored, and Thursday dawned with calm prevailing. Mayor Peters criticized both Curtis and Coolidge. President Woodrow Wilson, in Montana, wired that the strike was "a crime against civilization."

Coolidge called out the entire State Guard and issued a proclamation assuming temporary control of the Boston police and instructing them to take their orders directly from him. He then issued a general order dismissing the nineteen suspended policemen.

American Federation of Labor leader Samuel Gompers, just returned from Europe, sent Coolidge a telegram requesting reinstatement of the dismissed officers, to be followed by arbitration. Despite advice from supporters and political advisors that he should make concessions, Coolidge sensed that the moment was his. He replied to Gompers in direct, declarative sentences that included the statement that became national news: "There is no right to strike against the public safety by anybody, anywhere, any time."

Coolidge soon found himself mentioned as a potential Republican presidential nominee for 1920. His friend and supporter, Boston department store owner Frank W. Stearns, who had discerned Coolidge's leadership potential when the latter ran for lieutenant governor in 1916, wanted to begin organizing a campaign. Coolidge held back.

Meanwhile, Stearns published a collection of Coolidge's speeches in a book titled *Have Faith in Massachusetts* and distributed it widely to party activists. One recipient was Wallace McCamant of Portland, Oregon, who was impressed by Coolidge.

At the Republican National Convention in Chicago in June 1920, General Leonard Wood and Illinois governor Frank Lowden dueled for the presidential nomination through the first several ballots, with California senator Hiram Johnson trailing in third place. Then, a group of party leaders—mostly U.S. senators—met in a room in the Blackstone Hotel (later to be known as "the smoke-filled room") to settle on a compromise choice, Ohio senator Warren G. Harding. The word went down to the convention floor, and Harding was nominated on the tenth ballot.

The "bosses" also sent out word that Wisconsin senator Irvine L. Lenroot was their choice for the vice presidential nomination. After Lenroot's name had been placed in nomination and several seconding speeches made, Oregon delegate McCamant rose and placed Coolidge's name in nomination. The convention, chafing at dictation by the bosses, erupted in cheers, then nominated Coolidge.

In November, the Harding-Coolidge ticket defeated the Democrats' nominee, James M. Cox, and his running mate, Franklin D. Roosevelt, by 16.1 million to 9.1 million votes and 404-127 electoral votes. The Republicans had received a mandate.

President Harding invited Vice President Coolidge to attend cabinet meetings, an unprecedented move at the time. Nevertheless, Coolidge's duties as vice president were largely ceremonial.

Reading Coolidge's speeches from this period, one is struck by the care he took in writing them (he wrote his own speeches throughout his career). His knowledge and love of history are strongly evident. He frequently articulates his reverence for the Declaration of Independence and the U.S. Constitution and his conviction that they were God-given. In these speeches, he refined his longstanding themes of self-reliance, the value and dignity of work, the importance of spreading prosperity widely, and the need to operate government economically and tax the people only enough to do so.

On August 2, 1923, the Coolidges were vacationing at his family's homestead in Plymouth Notch, reassured that President Harding, who had fallen ill on a western trip, was apparently resting comfortably at the Palace Hotel in San Francisco. That evening, however, at 7:30 Pacific time, the president died suddenly. The news was telegraphed to Washington, then to Bridgewater, the nearest telegraph station to Plymouth. By now it was midnight. As the Coolidge home had neither electricity nor a telephone, the Bridgewater telephone operator drove to Plymouth Notch with the news. Coolidge's father, a notary, administered the oath of office to his son in the parlor of the small house, by the light of a kerosene lamp.

Once back in Washington, President Coolidge moved quickly to reassure the country that the

course of prosperity set by the administration would continue.

Initially, Coolidge kept the Harding cabinet intact. Probably the most important member of this cabinet was Andrew Mellon, secretary of the treasury, who had engineered important cuts in the marginal (highest) income tax rates. The federal income tax had been introduced in 1913 by Woodrow Wilson's supporters, essentially for the purpose of redistributing income. With the nation's entry into World War I in 1917, the tax was needed to produce revenue. The highest rate was seventy-seven percent. In Harding's first two budgets, Mellon had pegged the highest rate at fifty-four and forty-six percent, respectively. He believed that if marginal rates were perceived as too high, then economic activity—and thus Treasury revenue—would be impaired.

Coolidge worked with Mellon to promote tax policies that were intended to spur capital investment and economic growth. In his December 1924 annual State of the Union message to Congress, Coolidge said, "I am convinced that the larger incomes of the country would actually yield more revenue to the government if the basis of taxation were scientifically revised downward."

As if to validate that assumption, by 1927 seventy percent of income tax revenue came from "the rich" (i.e., people with annual incomes above $50,000). On the expense side, Coolidge also succeeded at federal budget balancing.

Unprecedented growth and prosperity ensued and continued throughout the remainder of his White House years. The nation's per capita income rose from $522 in 1921 to $716 by 1929. Automobile production went from 569,054 vehicles in 1914 to 5,621,715 in 1929. Sales of radios increased from a value of $10,648,000 in 1920 to $11,637,000 in 1929. The fledgling business of air travel went from 49,713 passengers in 1920 to 417,505 in 1929. The national debt, which had reached $26.3 billion after the war, was reduced to $19.3 billion by 1926.

Coolidge believed that, in normal times, the government should get out of the way, for the most part, and let the private sector—the people— build and expand economic prosperity. He said,

"I want the people of America to be able to work less for the Government and more for themselves. I want them to have the rewards of their own industry. This is the chief meaning of freedom."

British historian Paul Johnson, an admirer of the United States, described Coolidge's political philosophy as "minimalism" in government.

Coolidge believed ardently in the inherent value of free and open markets, but considered

material prosperity as only a means to an end—
the end being the enrichment of character and
spiritual values. In his speeches, he continued to
caution his audiences about the danger of consid-
ering prosperity as an end in itself ("Prosperity is
only an instrument to be used, not a deity to be
worshipped.")

The imagery that comes down to us from
Coolidge's "Roaring Twenties" era is one of
"Flaming Youth" and high living in the face of
Prohibition, but it scarcely applied to the majority of Americans. Such images drew media attention because they were "good copy" at the time
and later.

The decade of the Twenties was an era of
change, of a surge in technology based on electricity and the internal-combustion engine. The
number of patents issued between 1918 and 1934
was to be matched only in the late Eighties and
the Nineties. The stock of many famous compa-
nies first went on the market in the Twenties, sur-
vived the Depression, and produced great
amounts of wealth over the decades. Radio, and
its attendant advertising, promoted self-improve-
ment and beauty. Heroes and heroines captured
the public's imagination—Charles Lindbergh,
Admiral Richard Byrd, Amelia Earhart. Movies
were abundant and popular, as were their stars.

Calvin Coolidge was the antithesis of the popular image of the Roaring Twenties. He was the embodiment of thrift, industry, dignity, personal frugality, morality, and civility. He was respected, admired, and very popular. In the 1924 presidential election, Coolidge and running mate Charles Dawes of Illinois had 382 electoral votes, defeating Democrat John W. Davis and Progressive Robert LaFollette, who had only 136 and 13 electoral votes, respectively. (The popular vote was Coolidge, 15.7 million, Davis, 8.4 million, and LaFollette, 4.8 million.)

Critics of the Coolidge administration—especially the New Deal–era historians—contended that the prosperity of the Twenties was the result of stock speculation. Latter-day economists, however, attribute the great expansion of the economy to a combination of tax policies that encouraged investment, pent-up consumer demand following World War I, and a surge in technological innovation.

The critics reasoned that unchecked stock speculation during the Coolidge years led inevitably to the stock market crash of 1929 which, in turn, caused the Depression that lasted throughout the next decade. While stock speculation grew considerably in the 1920s, it is unlikely that more than one percent of the population engaged in it. (Today, by contrast, approximately fifty percent of Americans invest directly, and margin requirements are much higher.)

At the time, conservative financiers did worry about the growth in shares being bought "on margin." Typically, investors would put up only ten percent of the value of their purchase; the rest was borrowed from their brokers against the shares. Broker loans grew from less than $2 billion in 1922 to $6.5 billion in 1928. The Federal Reserve board worried about inflation. President Coolidge inadvertently encouraged continued speculation when, in January 1928, as a result of a press conference question, he issued a statement to the effect that the amount of money loaned by brokers was not too high.

When the stock market crashed in late October 1929, many speculators were wiped out because their margin loans were called and could not be paid. It should be remembered, however, that the large drops in stock value at that time were almost entirely reversed by spring of 1930. After that, a slow, steady market decline set in until the market hit bottom in June 1932.

During Coolidge's presidency, American agricultural interests had difficulty finding export markets for crop surpluses, but he blocked any bill or policy which he believed would inject undue government interference in agricultural markets. Although he foresaw the advent of widespread world trade, and even what was eventually to be termed "globalization," Coolidge did support tariffs to protect American manufacturers.

More than any other factors, the Smoot-Hawley Tariff Act (passed in 1930 after Coolidge left office) and subsequent tax increases were responsible for the acceleration of economic decline into the Depression. Smoot-Hawley imposed the highest tariffs in the nation's history and triggered retaliatory tariffs by other countries, resulting in sharp declines in U.S. exports. High taxes, imposed to replace lost revenues, aggravated the situation.

On July 7, 1924, Coolidge's younger son, Calvin, Jr., died of blood poisoning from an infected blister contracted during a tennis game. His death was devastating to Calvin and Grace Coolidge. Several historians have surmised that this led to Coolidge's decision in the summer of 1927 to announce that he would not seek re-election in 1928. His grief was certainly profound. He wrote, "When he [Calvin, Jr.] went the power and glory of the Presidency went with him."

Nevertheless, Coolidge did run for a full term that year, balancing his grief with his dedication to public service and a deep sense of duty. One may speculate that he felt he needed a full term to finish his work but, even by the summer of 1924, had decided he would not go beyond that.

When Coolidge left office in March 1929, the economy was continuing to grow. During his presidency, he had used the new communications medium of radio to spread his message broadly. He was the first president to broadcast his annual message (State of the Union) to Congress over radio. His 1925 inauguration was the first to be broadcast, as well. He made a number of radio talks from the White House. He was the first president to make systematic use of press conferences, with bi-weekly off-the-record meetings with the White House press corps, at which he was quite talkative.

Upon leaving office, Coolidge and his wife returned to their modest home in Northampton. In those days there were no post-presidential pensions, offices, and round-the-clock Secret Service coverage. The Coolidges lived quietly. He took an office in his old law firm, and his first project in retirement was to write his autobiography, in typically succinct Coolidge style.

In time, they bought a large home on several acres to insure their privacy (large numbers of the curious had been driving by his Massasoit Street duplex to catch a glimpse of him sitting on the front porch). The former president's only business engagement was to accept a position on the board of directors of the New York Life Insurance Company. He was elected president of the American Antiquarian Society, a position he enjoyed and carried out with enthusiasm. For one year, July 1930 through June 1931, he wrote a five-day-a-week newspaper column, reflecting on matters great and small.

During Coolidge's retirement, various visitors commented on the ups and downs of his energy and mien. He tired easily. On January 5, 1933, he died suddenly of a heart attack, at home. He was six months shy of his sixty-first birthday.

As president, Calvin Coolidge steered national policy in a way calculated to build a solid foundation upon which to expand opportunities for all Americans. Public service was his life's work and was rooted in his deep religious faith and convictions. ("Without the sustaining influence of faith in a divine power we could have little faith in ourselves.") Coolidge constantly called upon his fellow citizens to return to the fundamentals: work, leading to prosperity which, in turn, made possible more time for culture and the things of the spirit.

As Will Rogers observed, it all added up to "common sense."

A Calvin Coolidge Chronology

1872 July 4, born in Plymouth Notch,
Vermont, to John Calvin and Victoria
Moor Coolidge
Ulysses S. Grant re-elected president of
the United States

1875 April 15, sister Abigail born

1876 Rutherford B. Hayes elected president

1878 December 15, grandfather, Calvin
Galusha Coolidge, dies

1880 James A. Garfield elected president

1881 September 19, President Garfield assassinated; succeeded by Vice President
Chester Arthur

1885 March 14, mother dies
Grover Cleveland elected president

1886 February 22, enters Black River
Academy, Ludlow, Vermont

1888 William Henry Harrison elected
president

1890 March 6, sister Abigail dies (probably of
appendicitis)
May 23, graduates from Black River
Academy

1891 Late winter-spring, attends St. Johnsbury
Academy
June, certified to enter Amherst College,
Amherst, Massachusetts
September 17, enters the college as a
freshman

1892 Grover Cleveland again elected president

1895 June 26, graduates cum laude from
Amherst
September 17, engaged by Hammond
& Field law firm, Northampton,
Massachusetts, to "read" law

1896 William McKinley elected president

1897 Becomes a member for Ward Two of the
Northampton Republican City Committee

1898 February 1, establishes own law practice in Northampton
December 6, elected to the Northampton
City Council as one of three Ward Two
members

1900 January 18, elected by Northampton
City Council to be city solicitor
McKinley re-elected president

1901 January 17, re-elected as city solicitor
by city council
September 14, President McKinley
assassinated; succeeded by Vice
President Theodore Roosevelt

1902 January 16, fails at re-election by city
council for third term as city solicitor

1903 June 4, appointed clerk of the courts of
Hampshire County to fill a vacancy; does
not run in November for full term

1904 January, becomes chairman of
Northampton Republican City Committee
President Theodore Roosevelt elected for
full term

1905 October 4, marries Grace Anna
Goodhue, Burlington, Vermont

December 5, defeated as candidate for Northampton school committee (only ballot box defeat of his career)

1906 September 7, son John born (died May 31, 2000)
November 6, elected to Massachusetts House of Representatives, defeating incumbent

1907 January 7, takes oath of office as a member of the state House of Representatives
November 5, re-elected to Massachusetts House of Representatives

1908 January, begins second term in state House of Representatives
April 13, son Calvin, Jr., born
William Howard Taft elected president

1909 December 7, elected mayor of Northampton

1910 January 3, takes oath of office as mayor
December 6, re-elected to second term as mayor

1911 January 2, second term as mayor begins
November 7, elected to the state senate

1912 January, takes oath of office as state
senator
November 5, re-elected to a second
term in the senate
Woodrow Wilson elected president

1913 January 1, second state senate term
begins
November 4, re-elected to a third term
in the state senate

1914 January 7, elected and inaugurated
president of the Massachusetts State
Senate
June 28, Archduke Franz Ferdinand of
the Austro-Hungarian Empire assassinated in Sarajevo, triggering World War I
November 3, re-elected to fourth term
as state senator

1915 January, begins second term as state
senate president
September 21, nominated for lieutenant
governor of Massachusetts in Republican
primary
November 2, elected lieutenant governor

1916 January 6, inaugurated as lieutenant
governor

November 7, re-elected lieutenant
governor
President Wilson re-elected

1917 January, begins second term as lieu-
tenant governor
April 6, United States enters World War I
November 6, re-elected lieutenant governor

1918 January, begins third term as lieutenant
governor
November 6, elected governor of
Massachusetts
November 11, Armistice is declared in
World War I

1919 January 2, inaugurated as governor
February 24, welcomes President
Woodrow Wilson home from the Paris
Peace Conference, following the latter's
arrival at Boston by ship from France
September 9, Boston police strike
November 4, re-elected governor

1920 January 8, second inauguration as governor of Massachusetts
June 12, Republican National
Convention in Chicago chooses Coolidge
as the party's vice-presidential nominee

November 2, Harding-Coolidge ticket beats Cox-Roosevelt, 404-127 in electoral votes, 16.1 million to 9.1 million in popular vote

1923 **August 3**, takes oath of office as the Thirtieth President of the United States, the day after the death of President Warren Harding

1924 **June 12**, Republican National Convention, in Cleveland, nominates Coolidge for president
July 7, son Calvin, Jr., dies of blood poisoning from a blister developed after a tennis game at the White House
November 4, defeats Democrat John W. Davis and Progressive Robert M. LaFollette for presidency: 382, 136, and 13 electoral votes, respectively. Popular vote: Coolidge 15.7 million; Davis 8.4 million; LaFollette 4.8 million

1925 **March 4**, second inauguration as president; Charles G. Dawes of Illinois is vice president

1926 **March 18**, father, John C. Coolidge, 80, dies

1927 August 2, announces (in Rapid City, South Dakota, near vacation camp) that he will not stand for re-election in 1928, with famous statement, "I do not choose to run. . . ."

1928 January 16, addresses the sixth Conference of American States in Havana, Cuba

1929 March 4, leaves office; succeeded by Republican Herbert Hoover

1933 January 5, dies in Northampton, Massachusetts

THE QUOTABLE
CALVIN COOLIDGE

Sensible Words
for a New Century

African Americans

Numbered among our population are
some twelve million colored people. Under
our Constitution their rights are just as sacred
as those of any other citizen. It is both a public and a private duty to protect those rights.
Congress ought to exercise all its powers of
prevention and punishment against the
hideous crime of lynching, of which the
Negroes are by no means the sole sufferers,
but for which they furnish a majority of the
victims.

Annual message to Congress, December 6, 1923

Amending the Constitution

Our Constitution has raised certain barriers against too hasty change. I believe such provision is wise. I doubt if there has been any change that has ever really been desired by the people which they have not been able to secure. Stability of government is a very important asset. If amendment is made easy, both revolution and reaction, as well as orderly progress, also become easy.

Presidential address at the dedication of a monument to Lafayette, Baltimore, Maryland, September 6, 1924

America's Aspiration

America seeks no empire built on blood and forces . . . she cherishes no purpose save to merit the favor of Almighty God.

Presidential inaugural address, Washington, D.C., March 4, 1925

Americans—One People

Whether one traces his Americanism back three centuries to the Mayflower, or three years to the steerage, is not half so important as whether his Americanism of today is real and genuine. No matter by what various crafts we came here, we are all now in the same boat.

Presidential address to the American Legion convention, Omaha, Nebraska, October 6, 1925

Arms Policy

For the cause of peace, the United States is adopting the only practicable principles that have ever been proposed, of preparation, limitation and renunciation.

President's Armistice Day address, November 11, 1928

Banks

A bank is a not a private institution, responsible to itself alone, or to a few. It is a public institution, under a moral obligation to be administered for the public welfare.

Vice presidential remarks to a
New England bankers' dinner,
New York City, June 21, 1921

Baseball

We go to the game in the hope that with three men on bases the batter for our team will drive the ball over the fence so that we can revel in the intoxication of crowd delirium. That is the common touch of nature reaching from the street urchin to the President which lures us all to the ball field.

Newspaper column, October 3, 1930

Bewilderment

When people become bewildered, they tend to become credulous.

Newspaper column, November 28, 1930

Biography

Better wait till I'm dead.

From a conversation with historian Claude M. Fuess in Plymouth, Vermont, about a possible biography of the former president, August 6, 1932

Brevity

And be brief—above all things—be brief.

Second inaugural address as president of the Massachusetts Senate, January 1915

Business of the American People

It is probable that a press which maintains an intimate touch with the business currents of the nation is likely to be more reliable than it would be if it were a stranger to these influences. After all, *the chief business of the American people is business.* They are profoundly concerned with buying, selling, investing and prospering in the world.

Presidential address to the American Society of Newspaper Editors, Washington, D.C., January 17, 1925; the italicized phrase has been frequently misquoted as "the chief business of America is business."

Campaign Contributions

I do not like as a matter of principle large contributions given to campaign funds, because they create a bad impression and give the idea of a wrongful motive.

Remarks at a presidential news conference, April 24, 1924

Career Paths

If we would stop thinking that a bachelor of arts must be a white-collar man and let him be any kind of man he is adapted to be, the danger of spoiling a good craftsman to make a poor professional man would vanish.

Newspaper column, April 21, 1931

Centralization of Power

The centralization of power in Washington, which nearly all members of Congress deplore in their speech and then support by their votes, steadily increases.

Newspaper column, June 20, 1931

Change

In these days of violent agitation scholarly men should reflect that the progress of the past has been accomplished not by the total overthrow of institutions so much as by discarding that which was bad and preserving that which was good; not by revolution but by evolution has man worked out his destiny. We shall miss the central feature of all progress unless we hold to that process now.

Commencement address, while governor, at Holy Cross College, Worcester, Massachusetts, June 25, 1919

Character

Character is what a person is; it represents the aggregate of distinctive mental and moral qualities belonging to an individual or race. Good character means a mental and moral fiber of a high order, one which may be woven into the fabric of the community and State, going to make a great nation. . . .

Presidential address to the National Council,
Boy Scouts of America, Washington, D.C., May 1, 1926

Christmas

Christmas represents love and mercy. It was ushered in by the star of hope and remains forever consecrated by the sacrifice of the cross. Christmas holds its place in the hearts of men because they know that love is the greatest thing in the world. Christmas is celebrated in its true spirit only by those who make some sacrifice for the benefit of their fellow men.

Newspaper column, December 25, 1930

Civil Rights

The government of the United States is a device for maintaining in perpetuity the rights of the people, with the ultimate extinction of all privileged classes.

Presidential address in Philadelphia, September 25, 1924

Civilization and Profits

Civilization and profits go hand in hand.

Speech given in New York City on November 27, 1920, shortly after his election as vice president

Class Warfare

The attempt to appeal to class prejudice has failed. The men of Massachusetts are not labor men, or policemen, or union men, or poor men, or rich men, or any other class of men first; they are Americans first.

Statement to the press upon his re-election as governor, November 4, 1919

Classless Society

There are no classes here. There are different occupations and different stations, certainly there can be no class of employer and employed. All true Americans are working for each other, exchanging the results of the efforts of hand and brain wrought through the unconsumed efforts of yesterday, which we call capital, all paying and being paid by each other, serving and being served.

Speech accepting the vice presidential nomination, Northampton, Massachusetts, July 27, 1920

Common Sense

The people know the difference between pretense and reality. They want to be told the truth. They want to be trusted. They want a chance to work out their own material and spiritual salvation. The people want a government of common sense.

Speech accepting the nomination for the presidency, Washington, D.C., August 14, 1924

It has always seemed to me that common sense is the real solvent for the nation's problems at all times—common sense and hard work.

Interview with Henry L. Stoddard, December 14, 1932, in New York City; published in the New York Sun, *January 6, 1933, the day after Coolidge's death*

Compassion

Good government cannot be found at the bargain counter. . . . We cannot curtail the usual appropriations or the care of mothers with dependent children or the support of the poor, the insane, and the infirm. . . . Our party will have no part in a scheme of economy which adds to the misery of the wards of the Commonwealth—the sick, the insane, and the unfortunate; those who are too weak even to protest.

Campaign speech for lieutenant governorship,
Riverside, Massachusetts, August 28, 1916

To Edward K. Hall, in recollection of his son and my son who have the privilege, by the grace of God, to be boys through all eternity.

Coolidge's handwritten inscription in Hall's
copy of Have Faith in Massachusetts, *in memory of*
Hall's son, Richard, who died of polio at age nineteen
in November 1924, less than six months after the
death of Calvin Coolidge, Jr.; February 26, 1928

Conservation

Diminishing resources warn us of the necessity of conservation. The public domain is the property of the public. It is held in trust for present and future generations. The material resources of our country are great, very great, but they are not inexhaustible.

Speech accepting the vice presidential nomination,
Northampton, Massachusetts, July 27, 1920

Constitution of the United States

The more I study it, the more I have come to admire it, realizing that no other document devised by the hand of man ever brought so much progress and happiness to humanity. The good it has wrought can never be measured.

Autobiography, *1929*

Coolidge, Grace

A man who has the companionship of a lovely and gracious woman enjoys the supreme blessing that life can give. And no citizen of the United States knows the truth of this statement more than I.

Comment to friend, Bruce Barton, in 1926

We thought we were made for each other. For almost a quarter of a century she has borne with my infirmities and I have rejoiced in her graces.

Autobiography, *1929*

Country Life

Country life does not always have breadth, but it has depth. It is neither artificial nor superficial, but is kept close to the realities.

Autobiography, *1929*

County Fairs

The more modern and intricate forms of amusement are not able to detract from the wholesome pleasure that youth and age derive from the old-fashioned fair and cattle show.

Newspaper column, September 24, 1930

Courage

I won't pass the buck.

As governor of Massachusetts in 1920, Coolidge intervened in a bitter dispute between streetcar and jitney operators. When he ordered the railroads to put their streetcars back into operation, the jitney operators threatened to "crucify" Coolidge politically. "Don't let me deter you," he replied. "Go right ahead." Then he uttered the statement above.
Cited in Michael Hennessy's From a Green Mountain Farm to the White House, *1924*

Criticizing Others

I do not care to be criticizing those in power. If they succeed, the criticism fails; if they fail, the people find it out as quickly as you can tell them.

Interview with Henry L. Stoddard, December 14, 1932, in New York City; published in the New York Sun, *January 6, 1933, the day after Coolidge's death*

Declaration of Independence

In its main features the Declaration of Independence is a spiritual document. It is a declaration not of material but spiritual conceptions. Equality, liberty, popular sovereignty, the rights of man—these are not elements which we can see and touch. They are ideals. They have their source and their roots in religious convictions. They belong to the unseen world. Unless the faith of the American people in these religious convictions is to endure, the principles of our Declaration will perish. We can not continue to enjoy the result if we neglect and abandon the cause.

If all men are created equal, that is final. If they are endowed with inalienable rights, that is final. If governments derive their just power from the consent of the governed, that is final. No advance, no progress can be made beyond these propositions. If anyone wishes to deny their truth and their soundness, the only direction in which he can proceed historically is not forward, but backward toward the time when there was no equality, no rights of the individual, no rule of the people. Those who wish to proceed in that direction cannot lay claim to progress. They are reactionary.

Presidential speech in Philadelphia commemorating the 150th anniversary of the Declaration of Independence, July 5, 1926

Democracy

The light that first broke over the thirteen colonies lying along the Atlantic Coast was destined to illuminate the world. It has been a struggle against the forces of darkness; victory has been and is still delayed in some quarters, but the result is not in doubt.

Address as lieutenant governor at the home of Daniel Webster, Marshfield, Massachusetts, July 4, 1916

Diplomacy

The proposed visit of Secretary [Henry L.] Stimson to several countries in Europe reminds us that governments do not depend as much as formerly on the reports of diplomats, but are most disposed to take up important questions by direct personal contact between those in authority.

Newspaper column, June 5, 1931

Dogs

Any man who does not like dogs and [does not] want them about does not deserve to be in the White House.

Attributed by Roy Rowan and Brooke Janis in
First Dogs: American Presidents and Their Best
Friends, *Algonquin Books, 1997*

Duty

Do the day's work. If it be to protect the rights of the weak, whoever objects, do it. If it be to help a powerful corporation better to serve the people, whatever the opposition, do that. Expect to be called a standpatter, but don't be a standpatter. Expect to be called a demagogue, but don't be a demagogue. Don't hesitate to be as revolutionary as science. Don't hesitate to be as reactionary as the multiplication table. Don't expect to build up the weak by pulling down the strong.

Inaugural address as president of the Massachusetts Senate, January 7, 1914

Duty is not collective, it is personal. Let every individual make known his determination to support law and order. That duty is supreme.

Gubernatorial campaign address at
Tremont Temple, Boston, November 1, 1919

I felt at the time that the speeches I made and the statements I issued had a clearness of thought and revealed a power I had not before been able to express, which confirmed my belief that, when a duty comes to us, with it a power comes to enable us to perform it.

Commenting on his 1919 gubernatorial
re-election campaign in the Autobiography

Economic Policy

The wise and correct course to follow in taxation and in all other economic legislation is not to destroy those who have already secured success, but to create conditions under which everyone will have a better chance to be successful.

Presidential inaugural address,
Washington, D.C., March 4, 1925

Economic, Political Independence

There can be no political independence without economic independence.

Speech accepting the vice presidential nomination,
Northampton, Massachusetts, July 27, 1920

Economy in Government

After order and liberty, economy is one of the highest essentials of a free government.

Vice presidential speech,
Northampton, Massachusetts, May 30, 1923

I favor the policy of economy, not because I wish to save money, but because I wish to save people. The men and women of this country who toil are the ones who bear the cost of government. Every dollar that we carelessly waste means that their life will be so much the more meager. Every dollar that we prudently save means that their life will be so much the more abundant. Economy is idealism in its most practical form.

Presidential inaugural address,
Washington, D.C., March 4, 1925

Education

Education is to teach men not what to think but how to think.

Speech at Tremont Temple, Boston, as candidate for governor of Massachusetts, November 2, 1918

Education must give not only power but direction. It must minister to the whole man or it fails. Such an education considered from the position of society does not come from science. That provides power alone, but not direction. . . . I do not underestimate schools of science and technical arts. They have a high and noble calling in ministering to mankind. They are important and necessary. I am pointing out that . . . they do not provide a civilization that can stand without the support of ideals that come from the classics.

Commencement address, Amherst College, June 18, 1919

Courses of study must be pursued which require close application, accurate observation, precise comparison, and logical conclusion. I know of no courses which have supplied these requirements better than the study of mathematics, Latin, and Greek when they are supplemented by contemplation of the great truths of philosophy and a generous knowledge of history.

Remarks as vice president to the County Teachers'
Institute and School Directors' convention,
Reynoldsville, Pennsylvania, December 21, 1922

While it is easy to waste money on education, it is the one thing which we cannot afford to curtail. The true ideal would seem to be a system that supplies those in the lower grades with certain basic information and those in the upper grades with the power to think. . . . The school is not the end but only the beginning of an education. Yet its place cannot be filled in any other way. The best thing the millions of our youth can do to assure their future success is to work faithfully at their studies. That opportunity for improvement and discipline will never return.

Newspaper column, September 1, 1930

Eighteenth Century, Significance of

The Eighteenth Century was the era of the development of political rights. It was the culmination of the ideas of the Renaissance. . . . Custom was giving way at last to reason. Class and caste and place, all the distinctions based on appearance and accident, were giving way to reality. . . . The sovereignty of kings and the nobility of peers was swallowed up in the sovereignty and nobility of all men. The unequal in quantity became equal in quality.

Remarks on Bunker Hill Day to the Roxbury, Massachusetts, Historical Society, June 17, 1918

Enrichment of Life

There are two things necessary for the enrichment of life, mentally, physically, socially and spiritually. They are very simple and are known to all men. One is hard work and the other is a determination to do right.

Letter to H.W. Gibson, November 24, 1920

European Union

If Continental Europe can work out some plan for economic unity it will be of much profit to the world.

Newspaper column, May 18, 1931

Experts

Whoever deals with current public questions is compelled to rely greatly upon the information and judgments of experts and specialists. Unfortunately, not all experts are to be trusted as entirely disinterested.

Presidential address to the American
Society of Newspaper Editors,
Washington, D.C., January 17, 1925

F

Faith in God

Without the sustaining influence of faith in a divine power we could have little faith in ourselves. We need to feel that behind us is intelligence and love. Doubters do not achieve; skeptics do not contribute; cynics do not create. Faith is the great motive power, and no man reaches his full possibilities unless he has the deep conviction that life is eternally important, and that his work, well done, is part of an unending plan.

Presidential address delivered at the White House, July 25, 1924, and transmitted by telephone to New York to a delegation of Boy Scouts about to sail for an international meeting in Denmark; this occurred a little more than two weeks after the death of his own son, Calvin, Jr.

Family Farms

The family that makes the farm an old fashioned home with diversified crops, fruits and domestic animals sufficient to meet the household needs will still find agriculture one of the most satisfactory forms of existence.

Newspaper column, June 22, 1931

Fate

Fate bestows its rewards on those who put themselves in the proper attitude to receive them.

Autobiography, *1929*

Father

I think only two or three fathers have seen their sons chosen to be President of the United States. I am sure I came to it largely by your bringing up and your example.

Letter to his father, John C. Coolidge, August 2, 1925

Federal Intervention

Whenever some people find that abuse needs correction in their neighborhood, instead of applying a remedy themselves, they seek to have a tribunal sent on from Washington to discharge their duties for them, regardless of the fact that in accepting such supervision they are bartering away their freedom.

Presidential speech to the Daughters of the American Revolution, Washington, D.C., April 17, 1928

Federal Workers

Some prove incompetent. A very few are tempted to become disloyal to their trust. But the great rank and file of them are of good ability, conscientious and faithful public servants.

Autobiography, *1929*

Fishing

Now that the fields are growing green again the thoughts of many will be turned to the flowing streams. . . . The open country, the unhurried silence, the refreshing leisure are a stimulation to the body and a benediction to the soul. Even the imagination expands and the credulity is disciplined in telling and listening to adventures with rod and reel.

Praising the pastime he loved, especially at Plymouth Notch, in a newspaper column, April 6, 1931

Foreign Relations

We have a well-defined foreign policy. . . . It has as its foundation peace with independence.

Presidential address to the Chamber of Commerce of the United States, October 23, 1924

Ultimately nations, like individuals, cannot depend upon each other, but must depend upon themselves. Each one must work out its own salvation. We have every desire to help. . . . While we desire always to cooperate and to help, we are equally determined to be independent and free. Right and truth and justice and humanitarian efforts will have the moral support of this country all over the world. But we do not wish to become involved in the political controversies of others.

Message to Sixty-eighth Congress at the beginning of the second session, December 3, 1924

Freedom

I want the people of America to be able to work less for the Government and more for themselves. I want them to have the rewards of their own industry. This is the chief meaning of freedom.

Address accepting the presidential nomination,
August 14, 1924

The meaning of America is not to be found in a life without toil. Freedom is not only bought with a great price; it is maintained by unremitting effort.

"The Purpose of America," vice presidential speech
given at Johns Hopkins University, Baltimore,
February 22, 1922

There is no greater service that we can render the oppressed of the earth than to maintain inviolate the freedom of our own citizens.

Speech at Tremont Temple, Boston, as candidate for
governor of Massachusetts, November 2, 1918

Future

We review the past not in order that we may return to it but that we find in what direction, straight and clear, it points to the future.

Address as vice president, Burlington, Vermont, June 12, 1923

G

Gardening

It makes its appeal alike to youth and age. It is extremely practical on the one hand, and lends itself to the artistic on the other.

*Presidential remarks at the
National Conference on Outdoor Recreation,
Washington, D.C., May 22, 1924*

Directing the growth of plant life into orderly ways gives us a consciousness of working with nature which we cannot get from mechanics or commerce.

Newspaper column, April 22, 1931

Globalization

We must realize that our relationships with the outside world, already enormously important, will increase in number, complexity and importance in their influences on our social structure. We cannot begin too soon to prepare for this future.

Presidential address to the Association of the Land Grant Colleges, Washington, D.C., November 13, 1924

Governing

Let men in office substitute the midnight oil for the limelight.

Speech during campaign for lieutenant governor of Massachusetts, Essex County, September 4, 1915

Government is not, must not be, a cold, impersonal machine, but a more human agency, satisfying the heart, full of mercy, assisting the good, resisting the wrong, delivering the weak from any impositions of the powerful.

Address at first inaugural as governor of Massachusetts, Boston, January 2, 1919

Government cannot relieve from toil. It can provide no substitute for the rewards of service. It can, of course, care for the defective and recognize distinguished merit. The normal must care for themselves. Self-government means self-support.

Inaugural address as president of the Massachusetts State Senate, January 7, 1914

Government's Goal

The aim of our government is to protect the weak—to aid them to become strong.

Gubernatorial remarks on Labor Day,
Plymouth, Massachusetts, September 1, 1919

Government's Source

Our Government rests upon religion. It is from that source that we derive our reverence for truth and justice, for equality and liberty, and for the rights of mankind. Unless the people believe in these principles, they cannot believe in our Government.

Presidential remarks at the dedication of a
monument to Bishop Francis Asbury of the Methodist
Episcopal Church, Washington, D.C., October 15, 1924

Grant, Ulysses S.

There was no artifice about him, no pretense, and no sham.

Vice presidential remarks at the dedication of the monument to Grant, the eighteenth president, Washington, D.C., April 22, 1922

Greatness

The lessons of the war are plain. Can we carry them into peace? Can we still act on the principle that there is no sacrifice too great to maintain the right? Shall we continue to advocate and practice thrift and industry? Shall we require unswerving loyalty to our country? These are the foundations of greatness.

Inaugural address as governor of Massachusetts, January 2, 1919

Grief

When he went, the power and the glory of the Presidency went with him.

Writing about the death, in 1924, of his teenage son, Calvin, Jr. in the Autobiography, 1929

Hamilton, Alexander

The most conspicuous talent of this great man lay in his ability to put principles into practical effect. . . . In the affairs of a nation, especially of a free people, no one man is ever entitled to all the credit of a great accomplishment. But when it is recalled that it was the genius of Hamilton that conceived of a national government, that he played a leading part in the framing of the Constitution which established that government, that he was the chief author of the arguments by which it was commended to the several States for ratification, it appears probable that without him the American nation would not have come into being.

Vice presidential address to the Hamilton Club, Chicago, commemorating the anniversary of Hamilton's birthday, January 11, 1922

Health

Good health is one of our chief national assets. Yet, in spite of all the progress that has been made in the science of hygiene, the yearly losses in this country from the ravages of disease run into many hundreds of millions of dollars. The discouraging feature of the situation is that much of this is needless. . . . People give altogether too little attention to their health. They neglect to get sufficient fresh air and exercise. They are not careful enough about their diet. They overstrain their physical and nervous systems, with disastrous results. Because illness makes us a liability to ourselves, our family and our community, we all have a personal obligation to keep well.

Newspaper column, August 9, 1930

Home

Present conditions suggest this is a favorable time to build a home. The future may be better or worse, but the present appears good.

Newspaper column, July 21, 1930

Honesty

My conception of public duty is to face each problem as though my entire record in life were to be judged by the way I handled it,—to keep always in touch with the folks back home—to be firm for my honesty of opinion, but to recognize every man's right to an honest difference of opinion.

Statement in a newspaper advertisement, November 4, 1918, the day before his election as governor of Massachusetts

Honor

No person was ever honored for what he received; honor has been received for what he gave.

From a gubernatorial message vetoing a bill raising the salaries of Massachusetts state legislators by fifty percent, June 6, 1919

Horseback Riding

A horse is much company, and riding over the fields and country roads by himself, where nothing interrupts his seeing and thinking, is a good occupation for a boy.

Recalling boyhood days at Plymouth Notch,
Vermont, Autobiography, *1929*

Human Nature

Human nature remains constant.

Commencement address, while governor,
at Holy Cross College, Worcester, Massachusetts,
June 25, 1919

We must realize that human nature is
about the most constant thing in the universe
and that the essentials of human relationships
do not change. We must frequently take our
bearings from these fixed stars of our political
firmament if we expect to hold a true course.

Presidential inaugural address,
Washington, D.C., March 4, 1925

Human Rights

Men speak of natural rights, but I challenge anyone to show where in nature any rights existed or were recognized until there was established for their declaration and protection a duly promulgated body of corresponding laws.

Speech accepting the vice presidential nomination,
Northampton, Massachusetts, July 27, 1920

Humility

It is a great advantage to the President, and a major source of safety to the country, for him to know that he is not a great man.

Autobiography, *1929*

Idealism

We make no concealment of the fact that we want wealth, but there are many other things we want very much more. We want peace and honor, and that charity which is so strong an element of all civilization. The chief ideal of the American people is idealism. I cannot repeat too often that America is a national of idealists.

Presidential address to the American Society of Newspaper Editors, Washington, D.C., January 17, 1925

Ideals

There is no force so democratic as the force of an ideal.

Speech given in New York City shortly after his election as vice president, November 27, 1920

Equality, liberty, popular sovereignty, the rights of man—these are not elements which we can see and touch. They are ideals. They have their source and their roots in religious convictions. They belong to the unseen world. Unless the faith of the American people in these religious convictions is to endure, the principles of our Declaration [of Independence] will perish. We cannot continue to enjoy the result if we neglect and abandon the cause.

Governments do not make ideals, but ideals make governments.

Presidential speech in Philadelphia commemorating the 150th anniversary of the Declaration of Independence, July 5, 1926

Ignorance

It is characteristic of the unlearned that they are forever proposing something which is old, and, because it has recently come to their own attention, supposing it to be new.

Commencement address, while governor, at Holy Cross College, Worcester, Massachusetts, June 25, 1919

Immigration

Every race and creed that has come here in numbers has shown examples of unsurpassed loyalty and devotion to our country. But only by coming slowly, avoiding city colonies and spreading over the land do they arrive in the real United States. . . . We have certain standards of life that we believe are best for us. We do not ask other nations to discard theirs, but we do wish to preserve ours. . . . We reflect on no one in wanting immigrants who will be assimilated into our ways of thinking and living.

Newspaper column, December 13, 1930

Industry

Industry must be humanized, not destroyed. It must be the instrument, not of selfishness, but of service.

*Second inaugural address as governor of
Massachusetts, Boston, January 8, 1920*

J

Jewish Community

From earliest colonial times, America has been a new land of promise to this long-persecuted race. The Jewish community in the United States is not only the second most numerous in the world, but in respect to its old world origins it is probably the most cosmopolitan. . . . Every inheritance of the Jewish people, every teaching of their secular history and religious experience, draws them powerfully to the side of charity, liberty and progress.

Presidential remarks at the laying of the cornerstone of the Jewish Community Center, Washington, D.C., May 3, 1925

Justice

Let justice and the economic laws be applied to the strong, but for the weak there must be mercy and charity; not the gratuity which pauperizes, but the assistance which restores. That, too, is justice.

Vice presidential address at the Community Chest dinner, Springfield, Massachusetts, October 11, 1921

Just Teasing

Don't you think the road commissioner would be willing to pay my wife something for her recipe for pie crust?

To guests at their Northampton home, around 1914, after Mrs. Coolidge, who cooked little, had baked a particularly tough pie crust—the Coolidge housekeeper was ill.

Knowledge

Civilization depends not only upon the knowledge of the people, but upon the use they make of it. If knowledge be wrongfully used, civilization commits suicide.

Commencement address, while governor, at Amherst College, Amherst, Massachusetts, June 18, 1919

Last Words

Good morning, Robert.

Said cheerfully to the handyman at "The Beeches," Northampton, Massachusetts, January 5, 1933, as Coolidge prepared to go upstairs to shave. Minutes later, Mrs. Coolidge found him on the bathroom floor, dead of a heart attack.

Law

The observance of the law is the greatest solvent of public ills.

Speech accepting the vice presidential nomination,
Northampton, Massachusetts, July 27, 1920

Legislating

It is more important to kill bad bills than to pass good ones. . . . See that the bills you recommend from your committee are worded so that they will do just what they intend and not a great deal more that is undesirable. Most bills can't stand that test.

Advice to his father, who was about to become a state senator in Vermont, from Mayor Coolidge of Northampton, in a letter of September 6, 1910

Don't hurry to legislate. Give administration a chance to catch up with legislation.

Inaugural address as president of the Massachusetts State Senate, January 7, 1914

Let there be a purpose in all your legislation to recognize the right of man to be well born, well nurtured, well educated, well employed and well paid.

Inaugural address as governor of Massachusetts, Boston, January 2, 1919

Legislator's Pay Increases

When membership is sought as a means of livelihood, legislation will pass from a public function to a private enterprise. Men do not serve here for pay. They seek work and places of responsibility and find in that seeking, not in their pay, their honor.

From a gubernatorial message vetoing a bill raising the salaries of Massachusetts state legislators by fifty percent, June 6, 1919

Liberty

Liberty can be secured only by obedience to law.

From statement upon his re-election as governor,
November 4, 1919

Liberty is not collective, it is personal. All liberty is individual.

Presidential remarks to the Holy Name Society,
Washington, D.C., September 21, 1924

Lincoln, Abraham

In wisdom great, but in humility greater, in justice strong, but in compassion stronger, he became a leader of men by being a follower of the truth.

Gubernatorial proclamation commemorating Lincoln Day, Boston, January 30, 1919

He closed forever the great contest which had been waged for three-quarters of a century between the power of the States and the power of the nation.

Remarks while vice president in Springfield, Illinois, on the anniversary of Lincoln's birth, February 12, 1922

Lobbying

One of the hardest problems the Congress has to meet is the constant pressure of outside influences. . . . The organized minorities of special interests with agents and publicity bureaus for creating an artificial appearance of public opinion and showering Senators and Representatives with letters and telegrams have grown to huge proportions. . . . Almost all these organizations seek an expenditure of the taxpayers' money.

Newspaper column, December 1, 1930

Local Government

People are given to thinking and speaking of the National Government as "the Government." They demand more from it than it was ever intended to provide; and yet in the same breath they complain that Federal authority is stretching itself over areas which do not concern it. . . . Without doubt, the reason for increasing demands on the Federal Government is that the states have not discharged their full duties. Some have done better and some worse, but as a whole they have not done all they should. So demand has grown up for a greater concentration of powers in the Federal Government. If we will fairly consider it, we must conclude that the remedy is worse than the disease. What we need is not more Federal Government, but better local government.

Presidential address at Memorial Exercises,
Arlington National Cemetery, May 30, 1925

Luck

There are people who complain that they do not have any luck. These are the opportunists who who think that their destiny is all shaped outside themselves. They are always waiting for something to happen. Not only is nothing very good likely to happen to this class, but if some fortune seems to come it tends to turn out disastrously. They are usually ruined by success. Our real luck lies within ourselves. It is a question of character. It depends on whether we follow the inner light of conscience. . . . The man who is right makes his own luck.

Newspaper column, August 28, 1930

Management Style

When I pick out a man to do a job, I don't generally instruct him, but if you wish instructions, you draw them up and I'll sign them.

Upon Henry L. Stimson's acceptance, at Coolidge's request, of the post of Governor General of the Philippines, late September 1927; this reflects Coolidge's style of identifying a job to be done, selecting the person he thought best qualified to carry it out, then leaving that person alone to do it

Maple Sugar

Springtime is advancing up the valleys and slopes of the northern hills where old time country life still lingers. . . . The sugar season is opening. It is time to bring out the sap buckets and the great pans. . . . Then the maple trees will be tapped, the spouts set and the buckets hung. The dropping sap will make pleasant music, mingling with the cry of the blue jays and the complaining of the squirrels. . . . After noon the gathering of the sap begins. The great fire roars in the arch. The sap dancing in the pan sends clouds of steam to the tree tops. The air will be filled with the incomparable flavor of new maple syrup in the assurance the earth is again pouring forth her first seasonal bounty.

Newspaper column, March 18, 1931

Materialism

If material rewards be the only measure of success, there is no hope for the peaceful solution of our social questions, for they will never be large enough to satisfy. Men struggle for material success because that is the path, the process, to the development of character. We ought to demand economic justice, but most of all because it is justice. We must forever realize that material rewards are limited and in a sense they are only incidental, but the development of character is unlimited and is the only essential.

Address, as lieutenant governor, to the Brockton, Massachusetts, Chamber of Commerce, April 11, 1916

Material resources do not, and cannot, stand alone; they are the product of spiritual resources. It is because America, as a nation, has held fast to the higher things of life, because it has had a faith in mankind which it has dared to put to the test of self-government, because it has believed greatly in honor and truth and righteousness, that a great material prosperity has been added unto it.

Vice presidential remarks at
Fredericksburg, Virginia, July 6, 1922

Because of an endless struggle against the elements for the necessities of existence, it is natural to place great emphasis on material prosperity. While that attitude is proper and wise, we still should keep in mind that wealth is not an end but a means. We need it only for the use we can make of it. The real standard of life is not one of quantity but of quality; not of money but of character.

Newspaper column, August 8, 1930

Maturity

In the development of every boy who is going to amount to anything there comes a time when he emerges from his immature ways and, by the greater precision of his thought and action, realizes that he has begun to find himself.

Autobiography, *1929*

Memorial Day

The day is sacred to the memory of all the dead who wore our uniform. . . . They were the antithesis of selfish individualism, merging freedom and even chance of life in the common welfare of country. In danger, choosing the course that really counts, they preserved their rights by discharging their duties. No nation can live which cannot command that kind of service. No people worthy of such service will fail to do it in reverence.

Newspaper column, May 29, 1931

Military Preparedness

We have heard much of our lack of preparation. We have been altogether lacking in preparation in a strict military sense. We had no vast forces of artillery or infantry, no large stores of ammunition, few trained men. But let us not forget to pay proper respect to the preparations we did have, which was the result of long training and careful teaching. We had a mental, a moral, spiritual training that fitted us equally with any other people to engage in this great contest which after all is a contest of ideas as well as of arms.

On America's entry into World War I, from a June 17, 1918, address to the Roxbury, Massachusetts, Historical Society, commemorating the Battle of Bunker Hill

The only hope of a short war is to prepare for a long one.

Remarks as lieutenant governor to the Somerville, Massachusetts, Republican city committee, August 7, 1918

Money

Money will not purchase character or good government.

Address as lieutenant governor to the Brockton, Massachusetts, Chamber of Commerce, April 11, 1916

Morality

We are the possessors of tremendous power, both as individuals and as states. The great question of the preservation of our institutions is a moral question. Shall we use our power for self-aggrandizement or for service? It has been the lack of moral fiber which has been the downfall of the peoples of the past.

Address as vice president elect before the Vermont Historical Society; delivered in the Vermont House of Representatives, Montpelier, January 18, 1921

Mother

It seems impossible that any man could adequately describe his mother. I can not describe mine. . . .

Whatever was grand and beautiful in form and color attracted her. It seemed as though the rich green tints of the foliage and the blossoms of the flowers came for her in the springtime, and in the autumn it was for her that the mountain sides were struck with crimson and with gold.

When she knew that her end was near she called us children to her bedside, where we knelt down to receive her final parting blessing. In an hour she was gone. It was her thirty-ninth birthday. I was twelve years old. We laid her away in the blustering snows of March. The greatest grief that can come to a boy came to me. Life was never to seem the same again.

Autobiography, *1929*

Motivation

There are two fundamental motives which inspire human action. The first and most important, to which all else is subordinate, is that of righteousness. There is that in mankind, stronger than all else, which requires them to do right. When that requirement is satisfied, the next motive is that of gain. These are the moral motive and the material motive. While . . . they might seem to be antagonistic, yet always, when broadly considered or applied to society as a whole, they are in harmony. American institutions meet the test of these two standards. They are founded on righteousness, they are productive of material prosperity.

Vice presidential speech at Memorial Day services, Northampton, Massachusetts, May 30, 1923

National Security

No nation ever had an army large enough to guarantee it against attack in time of peace, or insure it of victory in time of war. No nation ever will. Peace and security are more likely to result from fair and honorable dealings and mutual agreements for a limitation of armaments. . . .

Presidential speech to the American Legion convention, Omaha, Nebraska, October 6, 1925

Nature

The silences of Nature have a discipline all their own.

Writing of the pleasure of long, solitary horseback rides in the Vermont of his youth; Autobiography, 1929

"New Deal," The

Great changes can come in four years. These socialistic notions of government are not of my day. When I was in office, tax reduction, debt reduction, tariff stability and economy were the things to which I gave attention. We succeeded on those lines.

Interview with Henry L. Stoddard, December 14, 1932, in New York City; published in the New York Sun, January 6, 1933, the day after Coolidge's death

News

The news, properly presented, should be a sort of cross-section of the character of current human experience. It should delineate character, quality, tendencies and implications. In this way the reporter exercises his genius. Out of the current events he does not make a drab and sordid story, but rather an informing and enlightened one. His work becomes no longer imitative, but rises to an original art.

Presidential address to the American Society of Newspaper Editors, Washington, D.C., January 17, 1925

Obvious, Importance of the

They criticize me for harping on the obvious. Perhaps someday I'll write On the Importance of the Obvious. If all the folks in the United States would do the few simple things they know they ought to do, most of our big problems would take care of themselves.

From "Back in Ward Four," by Coolidge's friend, advertising executive Bruce Barton, in The American Magazine, *March 1931*

Oratory

It would hardly be too much to say that since the dawn of civilization, the triumphs of the tongue have rivaled, if not surpassed, those of the sword.

Coolidge's first speech, "Oratory in History," at graduation exercises, Black River Academy, Ludlow, Vermont, May 1890

Patience

If one will only exercise the patience to wait, his wants are likely to be filled.

Autobiography, 1929

Patriotism

Patriotism is easy to understand. It means looking out for yourself by looking out for your country.

Vice presidential speech at Memorial Day services, Northampton, Massachusetts, May 30, 1923

Peace

Peace will come when there is a realization that only under a reign of law, based on righteousness and supported by the religious conviction of the brotherhood of man, can there be any hope of a complete and satisfying life. Parchment will fail, the sword will fail. It is only the spiritual nature of man that can be triumphant.

Presidential inaugural address,
Washington, D.C., March 4, 1925

Persistence

Nothing in the world can take the place of persistence. Talent will not; nothing is more common than unsuccessful men with talent. Genius will not; unrewarded genius is almost a proverb. Education will not; the world is full of educated derelicts. Persistence and determination are omnipotent. The slogan "Press on" has solved and always will solve the problems of the human race.

Written in retirement in connection with his membership on the board of directors of the New York Life Insurance Company

Pilgrims, The

Measured by the standards of men of their time, they were the humble of the earth. Measured by later accomplishments, they were the mighty. In appearance weak and persecuted they came—rejected, despised—an insignificant band; in reality strong and independent, a mighty host of whom the world was not worthy, destined to free mankind.

Vice presidential remarks at Plymouth, Massachusetts, on December 21, 1920, the 300th anniversary of the landing of the Pilgrims

Political Parties

There is no salvation in a narrow and bigoted partisanship. But if there is to be responsible party government, the party label must be something more than a mere device for securing office. Unless those who are elected under the same party designation are willing to assume sufficient responsibility and exhibit sufficient loyalty and coherence, so that they can cooperate with each other in support of the broad general principles of the party platform, the election is merely a mockery, no decision is made at the polls, and there is no representation of the popular will.

Presidential inaugural address, March 4, 1925

If a party is to endure as a serviceable instrument of government for the country, it must possess and display a healthy spirit of party loyalty.

Autobiography, *1929*

Party organization is necessary to the orderly process of self-government. It is truly representative. The only alternative is a personal and private organization that leads to boss rule.

Newspaper column, August 12, 1930

Politicians

The political mind is the product of men in public life who have been twice spoiled. They have been spoiled with praise and they have been spoiled with abuse. With them nothing is natural; everything is artificial. A few rare souls escape these influences and maintain a vision and a judgment that are unimpaired.

Autobiography, *1929*

It's a pretty good idea to get out when they still want you.

From a story related by Mrs. Coolidge in Good Housekeeping Magazine, *May 1935*

Politics

Politics is the process of action in public affairs. It is personal; it is individual; nothing more. Destiny is in you.

Politics is not an end, but a means. It is not a product, but a process. It is the art of government.

Essay "On the Nature of Politics" in
Have Faith in Massachusetts, *1919*

In a republic, knowing what ought to be done is different from knowing how to do it. The trained business man and experienced lawyer often fail in public life. Business buys what it wants and gives orders. The law demands its rights. Politics can only plead for support. It makes an appeal to a combination of a sense of duty and self interest.

Newspaper column, March 6, 1931

Power

I suppose I am the most powerful man in the world, but great power does not mean much except great limitations.

Letter to his father, John C. Coolidge, January 1, 1926

Presidential Legacy

Perhaps one of the most important accomplishments of my administration has been minding my own business.

Off-the-record news conference, March 1, 1929;
The Talkative President, *1964*

Presidential Statements

The words of the President have an enormous weight and ought not to be used indiscriminately. It would be exceedingly easy to set the country all by the ears and foment hatreds and jealousies, which, by destroying faith and confidence, would help nobody and harm everybody.

Autobiography, *1929*

Presidents

We draw our Presidents from the people. It is a wholesome thing for them to return to the people. I came from them. I wish to be one of them again.

Autobiography, *1929*

Private Sector/Public Sector Relationship

When government comes unduly under the influence of business, the tendency is to develop an administration which closes the door of opportunity; becomes narrow and selfish in its outlook, and results in oligarchy. When government enters the field of business with great resources, it has a tendency to extravagance and inefficiency, but, having the power to crush all competitors, likewise closes the door of opportunity and results in monopoly.

Presidential address to the Chamber of Commerce of the State of New York, New York City, November 19, 1925

Profits

Large profits mean large payrolls. But profits must be the result of service performed.

Inaugural address as president of the Massachusetts State Senate, January 7, 1914

We are dependent upon commercial and industrial prosperity, not only for the creation of wealth, but for the solving of the great problem of the distribution of wealth. There is just one condition on which men can secure employment and a living, nourishing, profitable wage, for whatever they contribute to the enterprise, be it labor or capital, and that condition is that some one make a profit by it. . . . It cannot be done by law, it cannot be done by public ownership, it cannot be done by socialism. When you deny the right to a profit you deny the right of a reward for thrift and industry.

Remarks as lieutenant governor elect to the Associated Industries dinner, Boston, December 15, 1916

Progress

Progress depends very largely on the encouragement of variety. Whatever tends to standardize the community, to establish fixed and rigid modes of thought, tends to fossilize society. . . . It is the ferment of ideas, the clash of disagreeing judgment, the privilege of the individual to develop his own thoughts and shape his own character that makes progress possible.

Presidential address to the national convention of the American Legion, in Omaha, October 6, 1925

Propaganda

Of education and real information we cannot get too much. But of propaganda, which is tainted or perverted information, we cannot have too little.

Presidential address to the American Society of
Newspaper Editors, Washington, D.C., January 17, 1925

Property

It is not property, but the right to hold property, both great and small, which our Constitution guaranteed.

Presidential inaugural address,
Washington, D.C., March 24, 1925

Prosperity

Prosperity is only an instrument to be used, not a deity to be worshipped.

Presidential speech given on June 11, 1928,
the day before the opening of the
Republican National Convention in Boston

The country is in the midst of an era of prosperity more extensive and of peace more permanent than it has ever before experienced. But, having reached this position, we should not fail to comprehend that it can be easily lost. . . . The end of government is to keep open the opportunity for a more abundant life. Peace and prosperity are not finalities; they are only methods. It is easy under their influence for a nation to become selfish and degenerate. This test has come to the United States. Our country has been provided with the resources with which it can enlarge its intellectual, moral and spiritual life. The issue is in the hands of the people.

Last annual message to Congress,
Washington, D.C., December 4, 1928

Prosperity, Dangers of

The trial the civilization of America is to meet does not lie in adversity. It lies in prosperity. It will not be in a lack of power, but in the purpose directing the use of great power. There is new danger in our very greatness. . . . It is impossible to overlook our imperfections. The war has greatly diminished the substance of some and greatly increased the substance of many. It has already given a new tongue to envy. Without doubt it will give a new grasp to greed.

Vice presidential address at the Community Chest dinner, Springfield, Massachusetts, October 11, 1921

Public Assets

What the public has, the public must pay for. From this there is no escape.

Address to the Republican State Convention, Tremont Temple, Boston, October 4, 1919

Public Debt

As I went about with my father when he collected taxes, I knew that when taxes were laid some one had to work hard to earn the money to pay them. I saw that a public debt was a burden on all the people in a community, and while it was necessary to meet the needs of a disaster it cost much in interest and ought to be retired as soon as possible.

Autobiography, *1929*

Public Opinion

Our government is a government of political parties under the guiding influence of public opinion. There does not seem to be any other method by which a representative government can function.

Speech accepting the vice presidential nomination, Northampton, Massachusetts, July 27, 1920

Public Service

The State is not founded on selfishness. It cannot maintain itself by the offer of material rewards. It is the opportunity for service.

Essay "On the Nature of Politics" in
Have Faith in Massachusetts, *1919*

Quoted, On Being

I don't recall any candidate for President that ever injured himself very much by not talking.

From a presidential press conference, September 16, 1924; The Talkative President, *1964*

You know, Mr. Secretary, I have found in the course of a long public life that the things I did not say never hurt me.

Recalled by Coolidge's secretary of war, Dwight F. Davis, for a series of articles in Good Housekeeping Magazine, *January-March 1935*

R

Racial Integration

It is true that the German high command still couple American and African soldiers together in intended derision. What they say in scorn, let us say in praise. We have fought before for the rights of all men irrespective of color. . . . It would be fitting recognition of their worth to send our American Negro [troops], when that time comes, to inform the Prussian military despotism on what terms their defeated armies are to be granted peace.

Remarks to the Somerville, Massachusetts, Republican city committee, August 7, 1918

Radio, Television, and Foreseeing VCRs

In its broad aspects radio is a new agency brought by science to our people which may, if properly safeguarded, become one of our greatest blessings. . . . With all its great possibilities, it is accompanied by a most intricate technology and a most intricate relationship to the Government.

The Administration . . . has from the beginning insisted that no monopoly should be allowed to arise. . . . What is required to meet this situation is an orderly process by which the opportunity for the use of radio communication can be kept open to the highest degree possible.

Presidential speech to the delegates of the Radio Conference, the White House, October 8, 1924

A new social force is being developed by radio waves. . . . Report comes simultaneously of a successful experiment in television by which people in Leipzig were able to recognize the image of a man in Schenectady. The time may not be far away when it will be possible to have a receiving set in the home that will produce a sound motion picture. . . . It is difficult to comprehend what an enormous power this would be. New forces are constantly being created for good or for evil.

Newspaper column, February 13, 1931

Re-election

If I should serve as President again, I should serve almost ten years, which is too long for a President in this country.

Statement in a conversation with presidential secretary, Chief of Staff Everett Sanders, Rapid City, South Dakota, in late July 1927; Calvin Coolidge: The Man From Vermont, *1940*

I do not choose to run.

Statement to the press regarding the 1928 presidential election; from Rapid City, South Dakota, while vacationing in the Black Hills, August 2, 1927

When I announced my determination not to run for President in 1928, my decision had been made a long time. While I wanted the relief that would come to Mrs. Coolidge and me from the public responsibilities we had held for so many years, my action was also based on the belief that it was best for the country.

Article in the Saturday Evening Post, *October 3, 1931*

Reform

Laws do not make reforms, reforms make laws. We cannot look to government. We must look to ourselves. We must stand not in expectation of a reward but with a desire to serve. There will come out of government exactly what is put into it.

Essay "On the Nature of Politics" in
Have Faith in Massachusetts, *1919*

Under a system of popular government there will always be those who will seek for political preferment by clamoring for reform. While there is very little of this which is not sincere, there is a large portion that is not well informed.

Presidential speech commemorating the 150th anniversary of the Declaration of Independence, Philadelphia, July 5, 1926

Religious Convictions

The foundation of our independence and our government rests upon our basic religious convictions.

Presidential address to the Holy Name Society,
Washington, D.C., September 21, 1924

Religious Teachings

Outside the teachings of religion there is no answer to the problems of life.

Newspaper column, April 3, 1931

Rights and Responsibilities

Let there be a purpose in all your legislation to recognize the right of man to be well born, well nurtured, well educated, well employed and well paid. This is no gospel of ease and selfishness, or class distinction, but a gospel of effort and service, of universal application.

*Inaugural address as governor of Massachusetts,
January 2, 1919*

Rockne, Knute

Knute Rockne is gone. . . . His activities had the benefit of publicity, but that does not account for his hold on young men. We shall find that in his constant demand for the best that was in them. No bluff would answer. Fifty per cent would not do. His passing mark was one hundred. He required perfection. That was why men honored and loved him. That was the source of his power.

Newspaper column, April 2, 1931

Roosevelt, Theodore

He appealed to the imagination of youth and satisfied the judgment of maturity.

Statement on the death of the former president,
January 6, 1919

Security

S

All through the ages people have been seeking some material security outside themselves. It has not yet been found. There is a possibility that the quest is a delusion. . . . In the end the security of nations and men must be sought within themselves by observing the command to do justice, love mercy and walk humbly.

Newspaper column, May 12, 1931

Self-Reliance

We demand entire freedom of action and then expect the government in some miraculous way to save us from the consequences of our own acts. . . . Self-government means self-reliance.

Newspaper column, October 17, 1930

Self-Righteousness

The world is made up of all kinds of people. Some are good and some are better, while others have made it necessary for the government to take charge of them. But it is a very hasty and ill-considered judgment to conclude that there is more bad than good in any one. We are all a combination of both elements. While we ought not to approve of the evil in ourselves or in others, if we should attempt to have no associations with any but saints, we should find ourselves very lonely.

Newspaper column, July 18, 1930

Sin

He said he was against it.

When asked by his wife what the minister had said in a sermon about sin; Coolidge Wit and Wisdom, *1933*

Social Welfare

We cannot curtail the usual appropriations or the care of mothers with dependent children or the support of the poor, the insane and the infirm.

Campaigning for lieutenant governor of
Massachusetts, Riverside, August 28, 1916

Spirituality

Statutes must appeal to more than material welfare. Wages won't satisfy, be they never so large. Nor houses; nor land; nor coupons, though they fall as thick as the leaves of autumn. Man has a spiritual nature. Touch it, and it must respond as the magnet responds to the pole.

*Inaugural address as president of the
Massachusetts Senate, January 7, 1914*

We live in age of science and of abounding accumulation of material things. Those did not create our Declaration. Our Declaration created them. The things of the spirit come first. Unless we cling to that, all our material prosperity, overwhelming though it may appear, will turn to a barren scepter in our grasp.

*Presidential speech commemorating the 150th
anniversary of the Declaration of Independence,
Philadelphia, July 5, 1926*

Sports

There is no better common denominator of the people. In the case of a people which represents many nations, cultures and races, as does ours, a unification of interests and ideals in recreations is bound to wield a telling influence for solidarity of the entire population.

Presidential remarks at the National Conference on Outdoor Recreation, Washington, D.C., May 22, 1924

Standard of Living

Some say we cannot go on maintaining a higher standard of living . . . than that enjoyed in other nations. We have done so for generations. . . . The theory that it cannot continue may be no better than the theory that it will last indefinitely. Some nation always has taken the lead. . . . Our example of a free and prosperous people has been the sovereign remedy for world oppression. The truth is our trade regulations are more fair to others than theirs are to us. . . . The higher our standards, the greater our progress, the more we do for the world.

Newspaper column, July 23, 1930

Stars and Stripes

He who lives under it and is loyal to it is loyal to truth and justice everywhere.

Gubernatorial proclamation in Boston on Flag Day, May 26, 1919

State Legislatures

State legislatures are fresh from the people. They know the conditions of their own neighborhoods much better than Congressmen know them.

Newspaper column, January 9, 1931

Strikes, Public Employee

There is no right to strike against the public safety by anybody, anywhere, any time.

Part of a September 14, 1919, telegram from Governor Coolidge to Samuel Gompers, president of the American Federation of Labor, regarding the Boston police strike

Success

The measure of success is not merchandise but character.

Speech before the Amherst College Alumni Association, Boston, February 4, 1916

Supreme Court

The safest place to declare and interpret the Constitution which the people have made is in the Supreme Court of the United States.

Address accepting the Republican presidential nomination, Washington, D.C., August 4, 1924

Talk

Let's spruce up a bit. And let's talk—it looks more natural and makes a better picture.

Comment to a friend as they were about to be photographed; Coolidge Wit and Wisdom, *1933*

Taxes, Tax Policy

I want taxes to be less, that the people may have more.

Remarks to a group of labor leaders visiting him in the White House, October 23, 1924

The collection of any taxes which are not absolutely required, which do not beyond reasonable doubt contribute to the public welfare, is only a species of legalized larceny.

The wise and correct course to follow in taxation is not to destroy those who have already secured success, but to create conditions under which every one will have a better chance to be successful.

Presidential inaugural address, March 4, 1925

Realizing the power to tax is the power to destroy, and that the power to take a certain amount of property or of income is only another way of saying that for a certain proportion of his time a citizen must work for the government, the authority to impose a tax upon the people must be carefully guarded.

Presidential remarks to the Business Organization of the Government, Washington, D.C. June 30, 1924

No matter what anyone may say about making the rich and the corporations pay the taxes, in the end they come out of the people who toil.

Presidential remarks to a group of labor leaders who called on him on September 1, 1924

Tax Exempt Securities

Another reform which is urgent in our fiscal system is the abolition of the right to issue tax-exempt securities. The existing system . . . acts as a continual stimulant to municipal extravagance.

Annual message to a joint session of the Senate and the House of Representatives, December 6, 1923

Teachers

It would be exceedingly difficult to overestimate the important part that teachers take in the development of the nation. They exercise their art, not on the materials of this world which pass away, but upon the human soul. . . .

Remarks as vice president to the County Teachers' Institute and School Directors' convention, Reynoldsville, Pennsylvania, December 21, 1922

Teaching

We have lost our reverence for the profession of teaching and bestowed it upon the profession of acquiring.

Commencement address,
Harvard University, June 19, 1919

Thrift

There is no dignity quite so impressive and no independence quite so important as living within your means.

Autobiography, *1929*

Thrift does not mean parsimony. It is not to be in any way identified with the miser. The thrifty person is one who does the best that is possible to provide for suitable discharge of the future duties of life. In its essence it is self-control. Contentment and economic freedom are its fruits.

Newspaper column, January 17, 1930

Time Off

I'm loafing, just rusticating.

*Said to the White House press corps while
visiting the family farm in Vermont during a
Congressional recess in August 1922*

Town Meeting, The

Each springtime sees it flourish all over
rural New England, whence it spread to other
parts of the nation. . . . No more effective
instrument for demonstrating the principle of
equality and liberty and teaching the art of
self-government has been devised.

Newspaper column, February 19, 1931

Troubles

If you see ten troubles coming down the road, you can be sure that nine of them will run into a ditch before they reach you.

Advice to President-elect Herbert Hoover in 1929; The Memoirs of Herbert Hoover: The Cabinet and The Presidency, 1920-1933, *1952*

United States as a World Power

We have taken a new place among the nations. The Revolution made us a nation; the Spanish War made us a world power; the present war has given us recognition as a world power. We shall not again be considered provincial. Whether we desired it or not this position has come to us with its duties and its responsibilities.

Address at Tremont Temple,
Boston, November 2, 1918

United States Senate

Its greatest function of all, too little mentioned and too little understood, whether exercised in legislating or reviewing, is the preservation of liberty. Not merely the rights of the majority, they need little protection, but the rights of the minority, from whatever source they may be assailed.

Vice presidential inaugural address, March 4, 1920

Universities and Colleges

They have served society because they have looked upon the possession of learning not as conferring a privilege, but as laying on a duty.

Address, Amherst College alumni dinner,
March 15, 1918

Unseen Values

We do not need more intellectual power, we need more moral power. We do not need more knowledge, we need more character. We do not need more government, we need more culture. We not need more law, we need more religion. We do not need more of the things that are seen, we need more of the things that are unseen. . . . If the foundation is firm, the superstructure will stand.

Vice presidential address at Wheaton College,
Norton, Massachusetts, June 19, 1923

Vacation

Rightly used it restores the vigor of mind and body by change and relaxation. We cannot always dwell upon the heights. We cannot always be at our best. If we are to do work of the highest excellence our periods of high activity must be followed by periods of rest.

Newspaper column, July 25, 1930

Vermont

Vermont is a state I love. I could not look upon the peaks of Ascutney, Killington, Mansfield and Equinox without being moved in a way that no other scene could move me. It was here that I first saw the light of day; here I received my bride, here my dead lie, pillowed on the loving breast of our everlasting hills.

In a short presidential address delivered from the rear of a train platform in Bennington, Vermont, en route from Wisconsin to Washington, D.C., September 21, 1928

Veterans

The nation that forgets its defenders will itself be forgotten.

Speech accepting the vice presidential nomination, Northampton, Massachusetts, July 27, 1920

Voting

Every voter ought not merely to vote, but to vote under the inspiration of a high purpose to serve the nation. It has been calculated that in most elections only about half of those entitled to vote actually exercise their franchise. What is worse, a considerable part of those who neglect to vote do it because of a curious assumption of superiority to this elementary duty of the citizen. They presume to be rather too good, too exclusive, to soil their hands with the work of politics. . . . Popular government is facing one of the difficult phases of the perpetual trial to which it always has been and always will be subjected. It needs the support of every element of patriotism, intelligence and capacity that can be summoned.

Presidential remarks before the Daughters of the American Revolution, April 14, 1924

We can secure a government of the bad by the good and avoid a government of the good by the bad only through the expression of the qualified voters. The cost to the people of enfranchised indifference is one of our heaviest taxes.

Newspaper column, November 1, 1930

War and Peace

We are against war because it is destructive. We are for peace because it is constructive.

*Presidential address at the annual luncheon of the
Associated Press, New York, April 22, 1924*

Washington, George

They [the 13 colonies] fought and won a revolutionary war . . . but the glory of military power fades before the picture of the victorious general, retiring his commission to the representatives of the people who would have made him king, and retiring after two terms from the Presidency which he could have held for life. . . .

Address, Amherst College alumni dinner, March 15, 1918

February 22 marks the . . . birthday of George Washington. His stature has only increased with the years. His public life was characterized by complete unselfishness. . . . He needed no pretense and no art. . . . From every avenue of approach we find a complete man. In all his actions he was precise, accurate, methodical. . . . It would be difficult to show him mistaken on any important question.

Newspaper column, February 20, 1931

Washington, D.C.

Its official circles never accept any one gladly. There is always a certain unexpressed sentiment that a new arrival is appropriating the power that should rightfully belong to them. He is always regarded as in the nature of a usurper.

Autobiography, *1929*

Wealth

Wealth is the product of industry, ambition, character and untiring effort. In all experience, the accumulation of wealth means the multiplication of schools, the increase of knowledge, the dissemination of intelligence, the encouragement of science, the broadening of outlook, the expansion of liberty, the widening of culture.

Presidential address to the American Society of
Newspaper Editors, Washington, D.C.,
January 17, 1925

Wealth comes from industry and from the hard experience of human toil. To dissipate it in waste and extravagance is disloyalty to humanity. This is by no means a doctrine of parsimony. Both men and nations should live in accordance with their means and devote their substance not only to productive industry, but to the creation of the various forms of beauty and the pursuit of culture which give adornments to the art of life.

Autobiography, *1929*

Welfare

The time has come when the people must assert themselves and show that they will tolerate no delay and no parsimony in the care of our unfortunates.

*Said during the campaign for lieutenant governor
of Massachusetts, at the home of Augustus P. Gardner
in Hamilton, September 1916*

White House, The

You have to stand every day three or four hours for visitors. Nine-tenths of them want something they ought not to have. If you keep dead-still they will run down in three or four minutes. If you even cough or smile they will start up all over again.

Advice to President-elect Herbert Hoover in 1929;
The Memoirs of Herbert Hoover: The Cabinet
and the Presidency, 1920-1933, *1952*

Wilson, Woodrow

He was moved by an earnest desire to promote the best interests of the country as he conceived them.

Presidential proclamation on the death of Wilson, the twenty-eighth president, February 3, 1924

Wit

Somebody did!

Coolidge's reply in 1898 to a man he had defeated for Northampton city council, and who had just exclaimed, "I don't know how you won, I didn't vote for you." Calvin Coolidge: The Man from Vermont, *1940*

Don't print that. It's really only $32, he might raise it on me.

Reply to a reporter, who asked Coolidge if it was true that he paid $35 a month rent for his Northampton residence; Coolidge Wit and Wisdom, *1933*

I've looked up the law, Senator, and you don't have to go there.

Coolidge's reply, as president of the Massachusetts Senate, to a plea for a ruling from a fellow senator, who had been told by a colleague on the floor to "go to Hell." Coolidge Wit and Wisdom, *1933*

I've been out of town.

Reply to a Northampton oldtimer who stopped Coolidge on the street during his first visit home after becoming governor, saying, "How d'ye do, Mr. Coolidge. I ain't seen ye about lately." Calvin Coolidge: The Man from Vermont, *1940*

You talk back.

Reply to Channing Cox, his successor as governor of Massachusetts, who had remarked that he was spending far more time in at the office than had Coolidge; Calvin Coolidge: The Man from Vermont, *1940*

Well, a man must eat.

Reply to Alice Roosevelt Longworth who had said to
him when he was vice president, "I guess going to all
those [dinner] parties must bore you. Why do you go?"
Memoirs of an Obscure Professor, *1992*

Call again.

Remark attributed to Coolidge upon a White House
messenger's delivery of his first presidential paycheck in
1923; Calvin Coolidge: The Man from Vermont, *1940*

You lose.

Attributed to President Coolidge by John Hiram McKee
and others, supposedly in response to a Washington
matron's declaration that "I made a bet today that I
could get more than two words out of you."

That's right. You stick to it. And I'll
amplify your statement by saying nothing.

Reply to the White House Secretary, who advised him
that a delegation was outside, insisting he had promised
to address their annual convention; the secretary had
told them they were mistaken, that it was not on the
president's schedule; Coolidge Wit and Wisdom, *1933*

Easier to control Congress than a college faculty.

Former President Coolidge's reply to a suggestion
that his name headed the list to become
president of Amherst College;
Coolidge Wit and Wisdom, *1933*

So did I.

Reply to a woman who had heard the former president
speak at Madison Square Garden and said,
"I enjoyed it so much I stood up all the time."
Coolidge Wit and Wisdom, *1933*

Women

What men owe to the love and help of good women can never be told.

Autobiography, 1929

Work

Work is not a curse, it is the prerogative of intelligence . . . and the measure of civilization.

*Remarks to the Amherst College
Alumni Association, Boston, February 4, 1916*

World Trade

Much of the criticism of the starting of foreign branches by our industries is short sighted. All the business on earth cannot be done within the confines of the United States.

Newspaper column, November 12, 1930

No one would be rash enough to try to estimate the probabilities of future world trade. But it is easy to see that from past development that it has possibilities that are very great. . . . The more it is examined the more nearly inexhaustible appears the opportunity for world production and exchange.

Newspaper column, February 16, 1931

Worship

It is only when men begin to worship that they begin to grow.

Vice presidential speech,
Fredericksburg, Virginia, July 6, 1922

Youth

Plenty of playgrounds and games is the best cure for youthful delinquency. Plenty of outdoor sports is a wise investment in good citizenship.

Newspaper column, September 12, 1930

Z

Zeal

The candid mind of the scholar will admit and seek to remedy all wrongs with the same zeal with which it defends all rights.

Commencement address, while governor, at Holy Cross College, Worcester, Massachusetts, June 25, 1919

Calvin Coolidge Archives

Calvin Coolidge is the last president for whom
there is no dedicated library for the collection of
his papers and memorabilia. These are to be
found in the repositories listed below. The Calvin
Coolidge Memorial Foundation provides detailed
descriptions of materials to be found at each site
in its publication *A Guide to the Coolidge
Repositories* (revised in 1998).

Calvin Coolidge Memorial Foundation
(Artifacts, ephemera, extensive archive of histori-
cal Coolidge photographs, reference library/files.)
P.O. Box 97
Plymouth, Vermont 05056
Tel. 802-672-3389. Fax 802-672-3369
E-mail: coolidge@vermontel.com
        info@calvin-coolidge.org
Web site: www.calvin-coolidge.org

**Amherst College Library,
Amherst Special Collections**
(Uncatalogued newspaper clippings, Coolidge's yearbook, correspondence from undergraduate years.)
Amherst College
Amherst, Massachusetts 01002
Tel. 413-542-2068, 2299. Fax 413-542-2692

Bailey Howe Library, Special Collections
(Material pertaining to Grace Coolidge.)
University of Vermont
Burlington, Vermont 05401
Tel. 802-656-2138

Baker Library, Special Collections
(Coolidge correspondence cataloged in collections of other individuals.)
Dartmouth College
Hanover, New Hampshire 03755
Tel. 603-646-2560

Black River Academy Museum
(Artifacts, ephemera, photographs—particularly of his high school days.)
14 High Street (P.O. Box 73)
Ludlow, Vermont 05149
Tel. 802-228-5050

Forbes Library, Coolidge Collection
(Papers and artifacts associated with Calvin
Coolidge and his family during the years he lived
in Northampton, 1895-1933.)
20 West Street
Northampton, Massachusetts 01060
Tel. 413-587-1014. Fax 413-587-1015

Historic Northampton
(Museum in three historic houses, interpreting life
of the region. Coolidge photographs, artifacts,
clothing, letters.)
46 Bridge Street
Northampton, Massachusetts 01060
Tel. 413-584-6011. Fax 413-584-7956
Website: www.virtual-valley.com/histnhamp

Library of Congress, Manuscript Division
(175,000 pieces of correspondence, mostly from
private citizens to President Coolidge, with car-
bon copies of replies; Coolidge destroyed most of
his personal papers from the White House years.
Also appointment books, telegraph messages.)
Washington, DC 20540-4680
Tel. 202-707-5387. Fax 202-707-6336

Vermont Division for Historic Preservation:
President Coolidge State Historic Site
Plymouth Notch Historic District
(Owns and administers some twenty-five buildings
and 1,000 acres at Plymouth Notch. Several buildings
have original archival collections from the late eigh-
teenth century to the early twentieth century, with
emphasis on the Calvin Coolidge years, 1872-1933.)
P.O. Box 247; Plymouth, Vermont 05056
Tel. 802-572-3773. Fax 802-672-3337
Website: www.cit.state.vt.us/dca/
                historic/hp_sites.htm

Vermont Historical Society & Museum
(Coolidge family papers, photographs.)
Pavilion Building
109 State Street
Montpelier, Vermont 05609-0901
Tel. 802-828-2291. Fax 802-828-3638
Website: www.state.vt.us/vhs/

Selected Bibliography

Books

Bollar, Paul F., Jr. *Memoirs of an Obscure Professor.* Fort Worth: Texas Christian University Press, 1992.

Coolidge, Calvin. *The Autobiography of Calvin Coolidge.* New York: Cosmopolitan Book Corporation, 1929.

—. *Have Faith in Massachusetts.* Boston: Houghton Mifflin Company, 1919.

—. *The Price of Freedom.* New York: Charles Scribner's Sons, 1924.

—. *Foundations of the Republic.* New York: Charles Scribner's Sons, 1926.

Coolidge, Grace. *Grace Coolidge: An Autobiography.* Edited by Lawrence E. Wikander and Robert H. Ferrell. Worland, Wyoming: High Plains Publishing Company, 1992.

Ferrell, Robert H. *The Presidency of Calvin Coolidge.* Lawrence, Kansas: University of Kansas Press, 1998.

Fuess, Claude M. *Calvin Coolidge: The Man From Vermont.* Boston: Little, Brown and Company, 1940.

Hoover, Herbert. *The Memoirs of Herbert Hoover, 1929-1941: The Cabinet and the Presidency, 1920-1933.* New York: The Macmillan Company, 1952.

Johnson, Paul. *A History of the American People.* New York: HarperCollins, 1997.

Kochmann, Rachel M. *Presidents: Birthplaces, Homes and Burial Sites.* Detroit Lakes, Minnesota: Midwest Printing, 1976, 1990.

Lathem, Edward Connery, ed. *Calvin Coolidge Says: Over 300 Dispatches Prepared by for-mer-President Coolidge and Syndicated to Newspapers in the United States and Abroad During 1930-1931.* Plymouth, Vermont: Calvin Coolidge Memorial Foundation, 1972.

---, ed. *Your Son, Calvin Coolidge: A Selection of Letters from Calvin Coolidge to His Father.* Montpelier: Vermont Historical Society, 1968.

McKee, John Hiram. *Coolidge Wit and Wisdom.* New York: Frederick A. Stokes Company, 1933.

Quint, Howard H. and Ferrell, Robert H., eds. *The Talkative President: The Off-the-Record Conferences of Calvin Coolidge.* Amherst: University of Massachusetts Press, 1964.

Roseboom, Eugene H. *A History of Presidential Elections.* New York: The Macmillan Company, 1958.

Silver, Thomas B. *Coolidge and the Historians.*
Durham, North Carolina: North Carolina
Academic Press, for The Claremont Institute,
1982.

Slemp, C. Bascom. *The Mind of the President.*
New York: Doubleday, Page & Company,
1926.

Sobel, Robert. *Coolidge: An American Enigma.*
Washington, D.C.: Regnery Publishing, Inc.,
1998.

Washburn, Robert. *My Pen and Its Varied Styles.*
Cambridge, Massachusetts: University Press,
1939.

White, William Allen. *Calvin Coolidge, the Man
Who is President.* New York: The MacMillan
Company, 1926.

—. *A Puritan in Babylon.* New York: The
Macmillan Company, 1938.

Woods, Robert A. *The Preparation of Calvin
Coolidge.* Cambridge, Massachusetts:
Houghton Mifflin Company, The Riverside
Press, 1924.

Journals, Proceedings

"Calvin Coolidge: Examining the Evidence"
(proceedings of a conference at the John F.
Kennedy Library), *New England Journal of*

History. Volume 55, No. 1, (1998). Waltham, Massachusetts: NEHTA, History Department, Bentley College.

The Real Calvin Coolidge, annals #2, 4-8, 10-14. Plymouth, Vermont: Calvin Coolidge Memorial Foundation, 1983-2000.

About the Author

The Quotable Calvin Coolidge is the sixth presidential book by Peter Hannaford. The others are *The Essential George Washington, The Quotable Ronald Reagan, Recollections of Reagan, Remembering Reagan* (co-author), and *The Reagans: A Political Portrait.*

He is also the editor of *My Heart Goes Home: A Hudson Valley Memoir* and the author of *Talking Back to the Media.*

In addition to his work as an author and editor, Peter Hannaford is a public relations/public affairs consultant. He resides in Washington, D.C., and the Mattole Valley in northern California.

IMAGES FROM THE PAST

Publishing history in ways that help people see it for themselves

THE REAL WOODROW WILSON: An Interview with Arthur S. Link, editor of the Wilson Papers
James Robert Carroll

Cold and unsmiling, idealistic but stubborn—these have been the popular images of Woodrow Wilson. In truth, he was a politician of considerable ability, an eloquent speaker, and a man capable of great warmth. A 1993 interview with Arthur S. Link, as he was concluding the 69th and final volume of the Wilson Papers after 35 years, reveals a fuller and more vivid picture of the president, and the compelling tale of Link's dogged perseverance, the joy of discovery, and marvelous luck. 28 illustrations. Chronology and bibliography.

5" x 7", 140 pages ISBN 1-884-592-32-5   Hardcover $19.50

THE ESSENTIAL GEORGE WASHINGTON:
Two Hundred Years of Observations on the Man, Myth and Patriot
Peter Hannaford

Why did Thomas Paine turn against him? Why did Elizabeth Powel call him "impudent"? What is the truth about the cherry tree story? What was his single most important quality? These and many more questions about the man called "the father of his country" are answered in this collection. The reader meets Washington's contemporaries, followed by famous Americans from the many decades between then and now and, finally, well-known modern–day Americans. Included are Benjamin Franklin, Thomas Jefferson, Abigail Adams, Parson Weems, Abraham Lincoln, Walt Whitman, Woodrow Wilson, Bob Dole, George McGovern, Eugene McCarthy, Letitia Baldrige, Newt Gingrich, Ronald Reagan—and many more. Read in small doses or straight through...either way, the book gives a full portrait of the man who—more than any other - made the United States of America possible. Over 60 prints and photographs.

5" x 7", 190 pages   ISBN 1-884592-23-6   Hardcover $19.50

WHITE FIRE
Stuart Murray

In 1828, frontiersman Dirk Arendt is guiding an archaeological expedition toward a lost city near Zululand when he learns that the leader of his party is an agent of a ruthless secret brotherhood. This agent is on a mission to find an ancient amulet said to be in the hands of Shaka, founder and lord of the Zulu nation. The amulet and its central Stone of White Fire—so named because it radiates a hypnotizing white glow—has the power to reveal King Solomon's fabled diamond fields and gold mines. More than that, say the legends, the amulet can bring great wisdom if used in the right way. If misused, it dooms its bearer to a life of torment. Dirk's expedition arrives in Zululand just as rebels are about to overthrow Shaka. The rebels, too, desire to possess the Amulet of White Fire as a token of Shaka's magic power.

Meanwhile, far to the southwest, the first Cape Colony pioneers (voortrekkers) journey northward into the wilderness in search of the Promised Land. These independent-minded folk include Dirk's own parents and an idealistic young woman, Rachel Drente. The trekkers do not yet know it, but the land they intend to settle on is rich in diamonds and gold just beneath its surface. The very wealth sought after by the secret brotherhood. Dirk and Rachel fall in love, but there seems little hope when they are caught between Zulu regiments and the conspirators who are seeking the Amulet of White Fire.

5 1/2" x 8 1/2", 325 pages ISBN 1-884592-25-2 Hardcover $26.00

WASHINGTON'S FAREWELL TO HIS OFFICERS:
After Victory in the Revolution
Stuart Murray

In the sunlit Long Room of Fraunces Tavern, on a winter's day in New York City, 1783, George Washington's few remaining officers anxiously await his arrival. He has called them here to say goodbye-likely never to see them again. The British redcoats have sailed away, defeated in the Revolution. This moving incident, one almost forgotten in American history, was among the most telling and symbolic events of the War for Independence.

As they anticipate their beloved general's arrival, the officers recall how their struggle for the sacred cause flickered, almost went out, then flared into final victory. In the story of Washington's Farewell are the memories of long-struggling patriots—the famous and the little-known—men committed heart and soul to the cause of American liberty: Knox, McDougall, Lamb, Hamilton, Steuben, Shaw, Humphreys, Varick, Burnett, Hull, Fish, Tallmadge, the Clintons, Van Cortlandt, Fraunces. . . . Heroes all. Index. Bibliography. 42 prints and maps.

5" x 7", 240 pages ISBN 1-884592-20-1 Hardcover $21.00

AMERICA'S SONG: The Story of Yankee Doodle
Stuart Murray

During the first uncertain hours of the Revolution, British redcoats sang "Yankee Doodle" as an insult to Americans —but when the rebels won astounding victories this song of insult was transformed to a song of triumph, eventually becoming "America's Song."

This is the first complete chronicle of the story of "Yankee Doodle," perhaps the best-known tune in all the world. From its early days an ancient air for dancing, through the era of Dutch and Puritan colonial settlement, "Yankee Doodle" evolved during the French and Indian Wars and the American Revolution to become our most stirring anthem of liberty. Index. Bibliography. Illustrated with 37 prints and maps.

5" x 7", 248 pages ISBN 1-884592-18-X Hardcover $21.00

RUDYARD KIPLING IN VERMONT:
Birthplace of The Jungle Books
Stuart Murray

This book fills a gap in the biographical coverage of the important British author who is generally described as having lived only in India and England. t provides the missing links in the bitter-sweet story that haunts the portals of Naulakha, the distinctive shingle style home built by Kipling and his American wife near Brattleboro, Vermont. Here the Kiplings lived for four years and the first two of their three children were born.

All but one of Kipling's major works stem from these years of rising success, happiness and productivity; but because of a feud with his American brother-in-law, Beatty, which was seized on by newspaper reporters eager to put a British celebrity in his place, the author and his family left their home in America forever in 1896.

6" x 9"; 208 pages; Extensive index. Excerpts from Kipling poems, 21 historical photos; 6 book illustrations; and 7 sketches convey the mood of the times, character of the people, and style of Kipling's work.

ISBN 1-884592-04-X   Hardcover $29.00   ISBN 1-884592-05-8   Paperback $18.95

THE HONOR OF COMMAND:
Gen. Burgoyne's Saratoga Campaign
Stuart Murray

Leaving Quebec in June, Burgoyne was confident in his ability to strike a decisive blow against the rebellion in the colonies. Instead, the stubborn rebels fought back, slowed his advance and inflicted irreplaceable losses, leading to his defeat and surrender at Saratoga on October 17, 1777—an important turning point in the American Revolution. Burgoyne's point of view as the campaign progresses is expressed from his dispatches, addresses to his army, and exchanges with friends and fellow officers. 33 prints and engravings, 8 maps, 10 sketches. Index

7" x 10", 128 pages   ISBN 1-884-592-03-1   Paperback $14.95

NORMAN ROCKWELL AT HOME IN
VERMONT: The Arlington Years, 1939-1953
Stuart Murray

Norman Rockwell painted some of his greatest works, including "The Four Freedoms" during the 15 years he and his family lived in Arlington, Vermont. Compared to his former home in the suburbs of New York City, it was "like living in another world," and completely transformed his already successful career as America's leading illustrator. or the first time he began to paint pictures that

"grew out of the every day life of my neighbors."
32 historical photographs, 13 Rockwell paintings and sketches, and personal recollections. ndex. egional map, selected bibliography, and listing of area museums and exhibitions.
7" x 10", 96 pages ISBN 1-884592-02-3 Paperback $14.95

LETTERS TO VERMONT Volumes I and II:
From Her Civil War Soldier Correspondents to the Home Press
Donald Wickman, Editor/Compiler

In their letters "To the Editor" of the Rutland Herald, young Vermont soldiers ell of fighting for the Union, galloping around Lee's army in Virginia, garrisoning the beleaguered defenses of Washington, D.C., and blunting Pickett's desperate charge at Gettysburg. ne writer is captured, another serves as a prison camp guard, others are wounded—and one dies fighting in the horrific conflict in the Wilderness of Virginia. Biographical information for each writer (except one who remains an enigma) and supporting commentary on military affairs. 54 engravings and prints, 32 contemporary maps, 45 historical photographs. Extensive index.
Vol. 1, 6" x 9", 251 pages   ISBN 1-884592-10-4
Hardcover $30.00   ISBN 1-884592-11-2 Paper $19.95

Vol. 2, 6" x 9", 265 pages   ISBN 1-884592-16-3
Hardcover $30.00   ISBN 1-884592-17-1 Paper $19.95

ALLIGATORS ALWAYS DRESS FOR DINNER:
An Alphabet Book of Vintage Photographs
Linda Donigan and Michael Horwitz

A collection of late 19th- and early 20th-century images from around the world reproduced in rich duo tone for children and all who love historical pictures. Each two-page spread offers a surprising visual treat: Beholding Beauty—a beautifully dressed and adorned Kikuyu couple; Fluted Fingers—a wandering Japanese Zen monk playing a bamboo recorder; and Working the Bandwagon —the Cole Brothers Band on an elaborate 1879 circus wagon. A-Z information pages with image details.

9 1/4" x 9 3/4", 64 pages   ISBN 1-884592-08-2 Hardcover $25.00

REMEMBERING GRANDMA MOSES
Beth Moses Hickok

Grandma Moses, a crusty, feisty, upstate New York farm wife and grandmother, as remembered in affectionate detail by Beth Moses Hickok, ho married into the family at 22, and raised two of Grandma's granddaughters. et in 1934, before the artist was "discovered", the book includes family snapshots, and photographs that evoke the landscape of Eagle Bridge, home for most of her century-plus life. Two portraits of Grandma Moses—a 1947 painting and a 1949 photograph, and nine historical photographs. On the cover is a rare colorful yarn painting given to the author as a wedding present.

6" x 9", 64 pages   ISBN 1-884592-01-5   Paperback $12.95

REMAINS UNKNOWN

Michael J. Caduto with sixteen pencil sketches by Adelaide Murphy Tyrol

The reader of Remains Unknown enters a world suspended between our earthly existence and the realm of the human spirit. This compelling tale is based on the true story of the body of a soldier from the Mexican War who died around 1860. His life is shrouded in mystery. Soon after the war, alone and restless, he began a long, tragic odyssey—a private purgatory that lasted over 150 years. For more than a century his mummified remains were used for research in two medical schools and a high school biology class. Long after death his spirit is held captive to this world.

One day, in the summer of 1997, a small community of people embarks on a mission of mercy to heal the wounds of a soul in pain and to honor the dignity of a human spirit. With the help of friends from Abenaki and Christian spiritual traditions, and a dose of healing humor in the face of grief, the journey unfolds with dignity and compassion.

5" x 7", 80 pages ISBN 1-884592-24-4 Hardcover $15.00

Available at your local bookstore or from Images from the Past, Inc., 888-442-3204 for credit card orders; PO Box 137, Bennington, VT 05201 with check or money order. When ordering, please add $4.00 shipping and handling for the first book and $1 for each additional.
(Add 5% sales tax for shipments to Vermont.)

www.ImagesfromthePast.com